Mathematics meets Technology

Brian Bolt

The right of the
University of Cambridge
to print and sell
all manner of books
was granted by
Henry VIII in 1534.
The University has printed
and published continuously
since 1584.

CAMBRIDGE UNIVERSITY PRESS

Cambridge
New York   Port Chester
Melbourne   Sydney

CAMBRIDGE UNIVERSITY PRESS
Cambridge, New York, Melbourne, Madrid, Cape Town, Singapore, São Paulo

Cambridge University Press
The Edinburgh Building, Cambridge CB2 8RU, UK

Published in the United States of America by Cambridge University Press, New York

www.cambridge.org
Information on this title: www.cambridge.org/9780521376921

First published 1991
Re-issued in this digitally printed version 2007

A catalogue record for this publication is available from the British Library

Library of Congress Cataloguing in Publication data
Bolt, Brian.
  Mathematics meets technology / Brian Bolt.
  p.   cm.
  Includes bibliographical references.
  ISBN 0-521-37692-0
  1. Kinematics.   I. Title.
QA841.B64   1990
621.8'11 – dc20   89–17458

ISBN 978-0-521-37692-1 paperback

For the purposes of this digital reprinting the commentary
section has been reproduced in black and white text.

Acknowledgements

The author would like to thank Tim Brierley who read
through the original manuscript and checked all the solutions.
Illustrations by Nigel Weaver

Photograph on page 73 reproduced by kind permission of
National Railway Museum, York.

Contents

Introduction

Since the industrial revolution we have been surrounded by a multiplicity of ingenious machines and mechanisms, a veritable treasure-house of examples of shapes interacting with other shapes in motion, whose study would give so much insight into spatial relations.

Technology in schools has changed beyond recognition in the last twenty years and has taken on board the study of mechanisms. However, technology has only been pursued by a minority of students. But the National Curriculum has put Technology alongside Mathematics as a core subject to be studied by all. This has opened up exciting possibilities for cross-curricular co-operation which this book has been written to promote.

Traditionally mathematics teachers have approached the teaching of geometry in a very static way, and even the introduction of transformation geometry in the sixties was largely abstract and seemed to have little relevance to the real world. But while this was happening the Schools Council was developing an enlightened Technology course on mechanisms which could so easily have complemented the new approach to geometry.

It was the move from a static view of space to the dynamic view afforded by teaching transformation geometry which for me sowed the seed of a whole new approach to teaching spatial awareness. In a search for ways of making 'motion geometry', as it was commonly called, meaningful I explored the working of machines such as car jacks, sewing machines, cycles and washing machines, and found that, not only were the students interested, but that it provided a stimulating source of geometric ideas. What also fascinated me about such a study was to find that the important spatial concepts concerned with moving shapes are often quite different to those which are traditionally emphasised. The geometry of moving shapes highlights other concepts than the theorems of Euclid.

Since the mid-1960s when I became aware of the important link between a study of space through movement (known as kinematics) I have taken every opportunity to explore this theme with teachers and students at all levels. I have also become aware of the long line of famous engineers and mathematicians who have strongly advocated a study of kinematics, and more particularly, a study of mechanisms.

Leonardo da Vinci (1452–1519) was probably the first person to systematically record a wide variety of mechanisms, many of which he is believed to have invented. Much later, at the start of the eighteenth century, the Swedish engineer Christopher Polhem produced detailed working models of the 80 basic mechanisms then known, and used them as a basis of a course in engineering design. Then Carl Cranstedt (1709–79), a pupil of Polhem, summarised his list of basic mechanisms in a sketchbook which he called his 'mechanical alphabet'. Towards the end of the nineteenth century Franz Reuleaux, a professor of applied mechanics in Berlin, compiled a mechanical alphabet of 800 models, while at about the same time Henry Brown, an American, published a book entitled *Five Hundred and Seven Mechanical Movements*. More recently, the great Russian authority on mechanisms, Ivan Ivanovich Artobolevsky, published five volumes on *Mechanisms in Modern Engineering Design*.

But none of this filtered down into our school curriculum until recently. Why? Is it because our courses have been too concerned with theorems, with proof, and with formal examinations? There is no doubt that a study of mechanisms cries out for a practical approach as Polhem and Reuleaux found, and this would not have found favour with the academic traditions of most mathematics departments.

In 1873, the Russian mathematician Tchebycheff wrote to Sylvester, the renowned English mathematician, urging him to take up kinematics as 'a very rewarding study which was more fruitful than geometry for it added a fourth dimension, that of movement'. Sylvester became obsessed by kinematics and spent much of his time extolling its virtues at public lectures in Britain and the USA. Kempe followed Sylvester as the great champion of kinematics in this country, but their lack of lasting impact was probably because their approach was academic and they failed to exploit the practical applications of the subject.

With more enlightened approaches to the curriculum and more imaginative forms of assessment pioneered by the GCSE and TVEI initiatives, the National Curriculum now gives opportunities to look at all our courses again, and in particular to develop links between Mathematics and Technology.

The industrial revolution has given us a wealth of examples of mechanisms to study, to analyse, and to classify, but with few exceptions the education system has been exceedingly blind to its potential. Modern machine shops and production lines with their use of robots, or farms with their modern machinery, rely on the imaginative application of the mechanisms invented in the last two hundred years, as does so much of the equipment in the home. When will we wake up to the possibilities inherent in their analysis?

This book has been written for teachers of mathematics and technology to help them to exploit the wealth of ideas in a study of mechanisms. A wide variety of mechanisms is discussed and illustrated by a range of applications, followed by a comprehensive set of exercises with their solutions.

How to use this book

This book has been written to give the reader an insight into the design of mechanisms as seen through the eyes of a mathematician. It can be used in a variety of ways. An individual could work through the book from cover to cover as a text book, but a teacher is more likely to use the book selectively, using it as a resource of ideas and activities to enrich his or her teaching of mathematics or technology. The exercises are extensive and an essential part of this book, but range in difficulty from activities which could be used with junior school pupils to those more appropriate to A level. To give some guidance, those questions and sections which are thought more appropriate to A level have been asterisked. Any further subdivision was thought to be unhelpful, for most of the questions not asterisked could be tackled by able children in a middle school by making appropriate models. Having said that, chapters 10, 11 and 12 are more suitable for secondary school pupils. Many of the questions repeat the same mathematical ideas but are seen in different contexts to help the reader appreciate their significance. Clearly, a teacher will use his or her discretion as to which questions from any given exercise to set. Some could be used as examples in an initial exposition of the topic and others set as assignments for the students to do.

Chapter 0 should be read first as it gives some essential background to all the chapters. The other chapters are largely independent of each other however and could be read in any order. Having said that, chapters 1 and 2 on rotary motion form a pair, while chapters 4, 5 and 6 are all on 4-bar linkages so would be better studied together.

To use the material in this book to its best advantage it is important that the practical activities are carried out. I often thought I knew what would happen without making and manipulating a model, but found that there were important aspects of the situation which did not become apparent until I had done so. If this was true of someone with years of experience of model making, how much more important it becomes to make models for those with little or no experience. It is only by handling linkages and gear trains that they are fully appreciated. There are many commercially produced gears and pulleys now produced at competitive prices, as well as plastic or metal strips for constructing linkages. A list of these is given at the end of this section, but much can be done at little expense by using card and paper fasteners, or click rivets.

There is a wealth of material here on the use of linkages which could be class taught, with pupils making up their own models to depict say a tool box, or a rocking horse, or a treadle sewing machine. By using card strips the pupils can then keep the models they have made, which is always an added incentive. In contrast, by using a commercial kit it would be expensive to equip a whole class and the models would need to be dismantled at the end of the lesson. However gear trains really require metal or plastic gears and a good selection can be purchased for a few pounds which will enable a group of pupils at a time to carry out practical experiments. This necessitates more of an individualised approach and work cards can be designed based on the questions in this book to suit the age and level of the group.

Using an individualised approach it would be possible to envisage a class working in groups on different chapters of this book at the same time and using it as a text book, with each group sharing a copy. However it would be better in the long term for teachers to use this book to inform themselves and then produce work cards appropriate to the groups being taught and the specific materials they have available and to their environment.

There are several aspects of a study of the mathematics of mechanisms:
1 models of basic mechanisms can be made and their properties investigated.
2 places where mechanisms are used can be observed and recorded.
3 a piece of equipment can be analysed to see the different basic mechanisms it employs and how they are interconnected. Where appropriate a working model can be made to illustrate the way the mechanisms work.
4 ways in which a specific mechanical problem has been solved can be studied and compared, e.g. the different design of car jacks, or pruning shears.
5 mechanisms which are designed to solve specific problems can be studied, such as a rotary switch to operate traffic lights in sequence, or a gear box with given ratios.

Another approach would be to take a mathematical topic as a starting point, and for the teacher to choose an aspect of the mechanisms to accentuate this, rather than study mechanisms in their own right. For example, the study of 4-bar linkages can be seen as an enlightened way of looking at quadrilaterals, while a study of the application of hydraulic rams to earth-moving equipment is all about the relationship between the angles and lengths of the sides of a triangle. In this vein, a study of robots is closely linked to using different co-ordinate systems for fixing a point in space and describing routes between points in space subject to various constraints. Much of the practical work will involve measuring lengths and angles, making scale drawings, producing loci, and drawing graphs. The work on pulleys and belts, sprockets and chains and gear trains abounds with applications of fractions, ratios, and directed numbers. In practice the combination of two transmission factors gives an excellent representation of the product of directed numbers.

This can perhaps best be understood from a table like the one which follows, which is illustrative rather than comprehensive.

Mechanism	Mathematical topic
4-bar linkage	quadrilaterals, parallelograms, trapeziums, angles, lengths, scale drawing, loci, graphs
variable-based triangle	scale drawing of triangles, use of cosine rule
hydraulic ram	volumes, ratios
levers	ratios, scale factors, enlargement
pulleys and belts	ratios, fractions, directed numbers, length of arc of circle
robots	co-ordinate systems 2D and 3D

Ideally a mathematics teacher would not work in isolation, but liaise with the teacher responsible for technology so that their work would complement each other's. In this way it would be easy to envisage joint projects which would draw from both areas of the curriculum. GCSE and TVEI with their emphases on course work projects and relevance give the possibility of developing this approach in a rewarding way.

To give an indication of the wide range of possible projects a list of examples is given below. When you have worked through this book you will find yourself becoming very aware of all the many mechanisms with which you regularly come into contact every day, but take for granted. Then you will have no difficulty in thinking up an endless list of project topics for yourself.

1 Make a study of folding push chair designs.
2 Design a folding bed which doubles as a settee.
3 Analyse the mechanisms in an upright piano. How do they compare with the corresponding mechanisms in a grand piano?
4 How does a mechanical typewriter operate?
5 Make a study of the apparatus in a children's playground and design a new ride suitable for young children.
6 Design a chair for helping people with arthritis to stand up.
7 Investigate the mechanisms in a piece of farm machinery and make a model to demonstrate how it works.
8 Investigate the design of a door lock, and make a model to show how it works.

9 Design a set of gears suitable for an all terrain bicycle.
10 How does a knitting machine work?
11 Describe the main mechanisms involved in a sewing machine.
12 Design an instrument for enlarging drawings in the ratios of 2:1, 3:1, 4:1.
13 Design a mechanism for a windscreen wiper so that the wiper blade oscillates through an arc of 120 degrees once every 2 seconds when driven by a motor that turns at 1200 rpm.
14 Design a moving picture book.
15 Design a chocolate bar dispenser which delivers one bar of chocolate for each correct coin entered.
16 Design a tin opening mechanism suitable for a disabled person who only has the use of one hand.
17 Make a study of an automaton and explain how it works.
18 Analyse the mechanism of a grandfather clock.
19 Analyse the transmission factors of different fishing reels.
20 Make a study of a fairground ride and explain the main mechanisms which give it its effect.
21 Design a mechanism for opening car windows.
22 How do refuse lorries operate?
23 How are car transporters designed to enable cars to be carried on two levels?
24 Make a study of the machinery in a textile mill and describe in detail the working of one of the machines.
25 Visit an old water mill and find out how the power is transmitted from the waterwheel to the mill stones.

Hardware resources

In recent years several companies have made it their business to supply kits and parts for making mechanisms, in a response to the growth of technology in schools. To anyone meeting this subject for the first time and who wants to teach it, it is suggested that the following companies are contacted to see the wealth of appropriate hardware now available.

Technology Teaching Systems Limited
Penmore House,
Hasland Road,
Hasland,
Chesterfield, S41 0SJ
Suppliers of: Lego Technic and Meccano kits and spares, books on technology.

Economatics (Education Limited)
Epic House,
Orgreave Road,
Handsworth,
Sheffield, S13 9LO
Suppliers of: Lego Technic, Meccano and Fischertechnik kits and spares, robots, hydraulic kits, books.

Automation Systems
43 Burners Lane South,
Kiln Farm,
Milton Keynes,
Buckinghamshire, MK11 3HA
Producers of an excellent range of parts and kits at competitive prices for a comprehensive study of mechanisms. For example, gear wheels are made with 10, 20, 30, 40 and 50 teeth in such a way that a wheel's diameter in millimetres corresponds to the number of its teeth.

Commotion, Technology Supplies
241 Green Street,
Enfield, EN3 7TD
Producers of Plawcotech construction kits with a wide range of gears, pulleys and parts for making up mechanisms. These kits have the added advantage that the parts are compatible with Fischertechnik, Lego and Meccano kits.

M W Models – 'Everything Meccano'
4 Grey Road,
Henley-on-Thames, RG9 1RY
A source of all things Meccano including magazines, kits and parts.

0 The background to a study of mechanisms

In our homes we are surrounded by mechanisms, from simple devices for fastening doors and windows, to cycles, lawnmowers, washing machines and cars. In the workplace typewriters, lathes, tractors, cranes or robots may be our everyday companions. What do they have in common? Can we analyse the wide variety of mechanisms we can observe in a meaningful way?

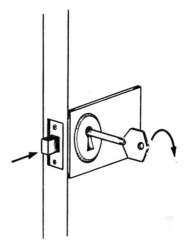

For a start, all mechanisms involve moving parts, and these parts interact with each other to convert one kind of motion into another, which may be similar or quite different to the original motion. The lock on a door is a good example.

When a key is inserted in a lock and turned, the bolt of the lock slides out or is withdrawn depending on the direction of the turn. In designing this mechanism the designer has to decide how far the bolt is to move, through what angle it is reasonable to turn the key, and then how one motion can be converted to the other. This is essentially a spatial problem. Other aspects of the design are concerned with the materials to be used, ease of manufacture, security etc., but are not the concern of this book.

In most mechanisms there is usually one part where the motion is initiated and another which does the useful work. Engineers have named these variously such as 'driver and follower', or 'master and slave'. Mathematically these can be compared to the input and output of a function or a computer, and you will be familiar with the sausage machine diagram used to represent a function which makes this comparison explicit. A mechanism transforms the input motion just as a computer processes the input data or a matrix maps ordered pairs.

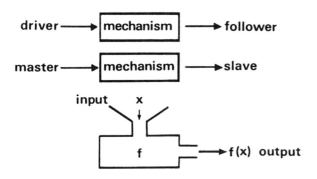

In this book the terms driver and follower have been adopted. For the lock mechanism above the key acts as the driver and the sliding bolt is the follower.

Another example is that of a glue-stick, or lipstick, where the driver is the end which is twisted and the follower is the stick of glue.

When analysing many mechanisms a key feature is the ratio of the angle turned through or distance travelled by the follower, compared with that of the driver, and this has been termed the *transmission factor*. This term incorporates and extends the more familiar term of gear ratio as used with gear wheels, by using directed numbers to take into account the direction of rotation. It also corresponds to the term velocity ratio as applied to pulley systems. It is a spatial feature of a mechanism which is determined by the shapes and sizes of the components which compose the mechanism.

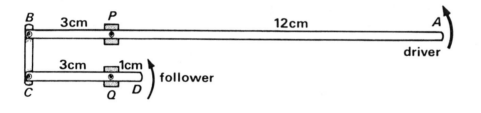

To appreciate the concept of a transmission factor and its multiplicative properties, consider the mechanism shown above consisting of three rods AB, BC, and CD which can turn freely about B and C, and about fixed pivots P and Q.

Suppose A is pushed through a distance of d cm, then B will move through a distance $d/4$ cm as $BP = AP/4$, so the transmission factor from A to B is $\frac{1}{4}$. This is denoted by $t(AB) = \frac{1}{4}$. Now $PBCQ$ is a parallelogram, so C will undergo the same displacement as B. It follows that $t(BC) = 1$. Also as CQ is $3DQ$, the transmission factor from C to D is $t(CD) = \frac{1}{3}$. Further consideration shows that the overall transmission factor from A to D will be given by the product of the individual transmission factors, so

$$t(AD) = t(AB) \times t(BC) \times t(CD) = \frac{1}{4} \times 1 \times \frac{1}{3} = \frac{1}{12}.$$

This type of analysis features in many of the following chapters and is critical to the understanding of many mechanisms.

1 Around we go!

Transmitting rotary motion using belts, pulleys, sprockets and chains

In many machines today the *driver* is an electric motor which powers one shaft to turn at a fixed speed while the *follower*, such as the rotating drum of a washing machine or the blades of a liquidiser or the hands of a clock, turns at a different fixed speed. There are several ways in which this transmission can be achieved but they all have common features.

Pulleys and belts

If you have ever visited an old textile mill or bobbin mill or seen photos of machine shops from the 1900s you will have been impressed by the array of shafts and pulleys overhead rotating at high speed and linked by flapping belts to every machine in sight. Treadle sewing machines used a belt drive from the flywheel which doubled as a pulley, and when the treadle was replaced by an electric motor a belt was again in evidence. Electric lawn mowers and upright vacuum cleaners also make use of a belt drive as anyone using them will be aware, for it is the part which wears out first and needs replacing. Car engines all have a 'fan belt' which has the dual purpose of linking the crankshaft of the engine to the fan to keep the engine cool, and to the alternator to charge the battery.

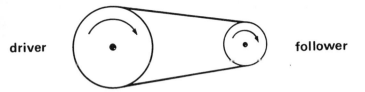

driver   follower

What we need to know is the angle of rotation of the follower compared to that of the driver and how it relates to the sizes of the pulleys. With a simple arrangement like that shown:

$$\frac{\text{angle of rotation of } B}{\text{angle of rotation of } A} = \frac{\text{diameter of } A}{\text{diameter of } B}$$

This is not at all obvious to many people and yet it is a fundamental concept which should be appreciated. To understand this relationship practical experience with simple models is the answer. They need not be elaborate. Pieces of dowel, pencils and cotton reels can be used for shafts and pulleys and rubber bands as belts, although more convincing models can be constructed from commercial construction kits such as Meccano or Fischertechnik. But it would not be difficult for schools' technology departments to cut out some plywood discs with diameters of say 4 cm, 8 cm, 12 cm and 16 cm to experiment with.

Initially it is important to realise that when the diameter of A is larger than that of B, then B will turn further than A, and vice versa. The next step is to determine the ratio of the angles turned through, and this is best approached by seeing the angle turned through by B when A makes one revolution. Then arguments can be based on how far the belt moves along its own length, which makes a direct link with the diameters of the pulleys.

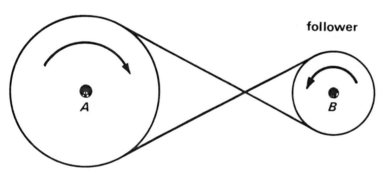

By crossing the belt over as shown above the ratio of the angles turned through will be as before, but this time B will turn in the opposite direction to A. To distinguish between these ratios it is helpful to have the concept of a *transmission factor* defined as follows:

$$\text{transmission factor from } A \text{ to } B = \frac{\text{angle turned by } B}{\text{angle turned by } A}$$

This will be a positive number when the shafts turn in the same direction and a negative number when they turn in opposite directions. As well as the definition it is useful to have a notation and we shall use $t(AB)$ for the *transmission factor* from A to B.

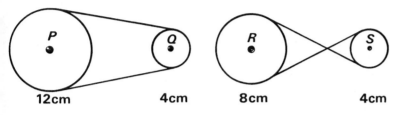

12cm   4cm   8cm   4cm

Thus in the examples above, where the measurements correspond to the diameters of the pulleys,

$t(PQ) = +3$ and $t(RS) = -2$

What are $t(QP)$ and $t(SR)$?

In general it is important to realise that

$$t(BA) = 1/t(AB)$$

Using two pulleys it is theoretically possible to obtain a transmission factor equal to any real number, as large or as small as required. In practice, however, there is a practical limit to the sizes of the pulleys. If they are too small the belt has a tendency to slip and if they are too large they just take up too much room. A transmission factor of $+15$ can be obtained, for example, by having the driver with a diameter of 60 cm and the follower with a diameter of 4 cm. But suppose we can only obtain pulleys in the range 4 cm to 20 cm in steps of 4 cm. How can we obtain a transmission factor of $|15$?

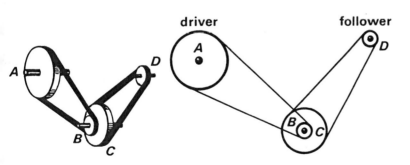

driver   follower

5

The solution to this design problem is to be found in the system of pulleys and belts shown on page 5. If A has a diameter of 20 cm and B a diameter of 4 cm then $t(AB) = +5$. Now take pulley C with a diameter of 12 cm and fix it to the same shaft as B so that they turn together, and let pulley D have a diameter of 4 cm, then $t(CD) = +3$. But for each complete turn of A, both B and C turn through 5 revolutions so D will turn through $5 \times 3 = 15$ revolutions. The result is that $t(AD) = +15$.

In general, the effect of combining two single pulley systems in this way, with the follower of one system being on the same shaft as the driver of the next, is that the overall transmission factor is the product of the individual transmission factors. This can be summarised as

$$t(AD) = t(AB) \times t(CD)$$

but may be more satisfactorily seen as

$$t(AD) = t(AB) \times t(BC) \times t(CD)$$

where $t(BC) = +1$ due to the pulleys being fixed to the same shaft.

The algebra of transmission factors is identical to the multiplication of the real numbers. Because of this it affords an excellent illustration of the product of directed numbers as the examples below illustrate.

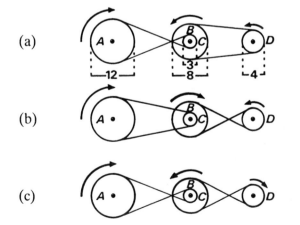

(a) $\qquad t(AD) = t(AB) \times t(CD) = -4 \times +2 = -8$

(b) $\qquad t(AD) = t(AB) \times t(CD) = +4 \times -2 = -8$

(c) $\qquad t(AD) = t(AB) \times t(CD) = -4 \times -2 = +8$

On some machines such as lathes and drills it is necessary to provide for a range of speeds. This is often done by arranging two blocks of pulleys as shown in the figure on the right.

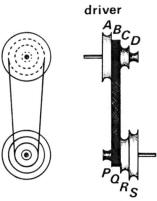

driver

follower

These are known as stepped cone pulleys for obvious reasons. Depending on the position of the belt the follower will turn faster or slower than the drive shaft.

If the diameters of the pulleys are stepped from 6 cm to 12 cm in 2 cm intervals then the four available transmission factors are

$$t(AP) = \frac{12}{6} = +2$$

$$t(BQ) = \frac{10}{8} = +1.25$$

$$t(CR) = \frac{8}{10} = +0.8$$

$$t(DS) = \frac{6}{12} = +0.5$$

The earliest cars used belts and pulleys to transmit the power from the engine to the driving wheels but this was replaced by gears (see chapter 2) because of the frequent failure of the belts. Now, however, with the improvement in belt technology, there has been a resurgence of interest in bringing back belt drive to family cars. First Daf and then Volvo, Ford and Fiat have replaced the gearbox in some of their cars by an automatic continuously variable gear based on the development of the stepped pulley block. Instead of a block of pulleys of different sizes, imagine the pulley being replaced by a cone (see below).

With the belt at the left-hand end of the cones, a small diameter drives a large diameter which is the lowest transmission factor available. As the belt is moved from left to right, the effective diameter of the driver increases and that of the follower decreases so that the transmission factor steadily increases. This mechanism enables a car's speed to be changed by changing the gear while leaving the engine speed unchanged. This is more efficient than the use of a traditional gearbox where the change in a car's speed can only be brought about by a change in the engine's speed. With their 'Variomatic' transmission Volvo are able to produce a top gear which is 4 times as high as the lowest gear, while Ford claims that its automatic transmission has a range which could only be matched by a six-speed manual gearbox. So this breakthrough in design has not only produced a continuously variable transmission factor but a much wider range compared to existing gearboxes. The effect is to allow the engine to be run at its most efficient speed. While cruising at 110 km/h, for example, the engine turns at little more than 2500 rpm.

driver

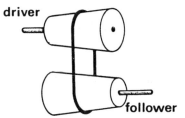

follower

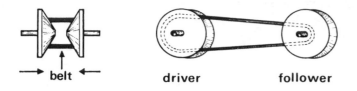

belt ← driver follower

In practice, the design of each 'pulley' consists of two frustums of cones which can be moved towards or away from each other, thus forcing the belt to take up a position further away or closer to the drive shaft. If the conditions require a lower gear, then the two halves of the driver pulley move outwards, reducing its effective diameter, while the two halves of the follower are forced together to increase its diameter. A higher gear is obtained by doing the opposite.

Sprockets and chains

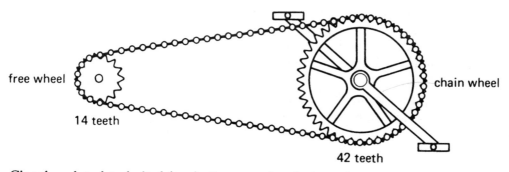

free wheel

14 teeth

chain wheel

42 teeth

Closely related to belt drive is the use of a chain and sprockets. This is familiar to everyone in its use for transmitting the movement of the pedals of a bicycle to the rear wheel. But what few people realise is the significant breakthrough in cycle design this mechanism brought about. Prior to 1885, when Starley introduced chain drive to his Rover Safety Bicycle, all bicycles used direct drive. The pedals were linked directly to the driving wheel as in a child's tricycle or a penny-farthing, so that one turn of the pedals gave one turn of the driving wheel. The bicycle would thus move forward a distance equal to the circumference of the driving wheel for each turn of the pedals, and the gear of the bicycle was entirely dependent on the size of the driving wheel.

Even with a large driving wheel as in a penny-farthing, the effective gear was low compared to a modern bicycle. Using a chain wheel with 42 teeth (see page 8) and a free wheel with 14 teeth, the chain will turn the free wheel, and hence the rear wheel of the bicycle, through 3 turns for every turn of the pedals. A typical bicycle has wheels of 69 cm (27 in) diameter so one turn of the pedals would take the bicycle the same distance as a penny-farthing with a driving wheel of diameter $3 \times 69 = 207$ cm (81 in). A little consideration would soon convince you that no living person could sit astride a penny-farthing with a wheel of this size and push its pedals, for it would require an inner leg measurement of at least 127 cm (50 in)!

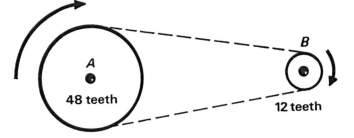

To calculate the transmission factor for two shafts related by sprockets and a chain, all that is necessary is to take the ratio of the numbers of teeth on the sprockets. In the example above (note the convention for representing a chain by a dashed line to distinguish it from a belt)

$$t(AB) = \frac{\text{number of teeth on sprocket } A}{\text{number of teeth on sprocket } B} = \frac{48}{12} = +4$$

One way to appreciate this is to realise that one revolution of A will move the chain 48 links along its length and this will rotate sprocket B, with 12 teeth, through 4 complete turns. To establish this concept experiments can be carried out using a range of bicycles or making use of construction kits such as Meccano or Fischertechnik.

There is plenty of scope with bicycles for comparing gears by relating them all to the size of the driving wheel of the equivalent penny-farthing, and this is how professional cyclists measure their gears:

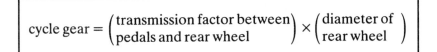

$$\text{cycle gear} = \left(\begin{array}{l}\text{transmission factor between} \\ \text{pedals and rear wheel}\end{array}\right) \times \left(\begin{array}{l}\text{diameter of} \\ \text{rear wheel}\end{array}\right)$$

Racing cyclists use gears where there is a block of 5 sprockets of different sizes connected to the rear wheel and two different sized chain wheels (a double clanger). A chain links one of the chain wheels to one of the free wheel sprockets and the rider has control of mechanisms to move the chain sideways to engage different sprockets. On a typical bicycle, the number of teeth on the free wheel sprockets range from 14 to 28 and the sprockets on the chain wheels have 32 teeth and 50 teeth. The highest and lowest transmission factors available are thus given by

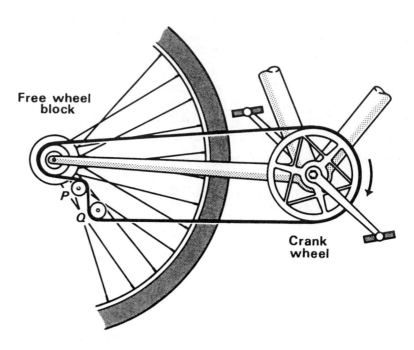

Free wheel block

Crank wheel

$$\text{highest t.f.} = \frac{50}{14} \qquad \text{lowest t.f.} = \frac{32}{28}$$

so with a 27 inch wheel the gears range from

$$\frac{50}{14} \times 27 = 96.4 \text{ inches}$$

to $\quad \frac{32}{28} \times 27 = 30.9 \text{ inches}$

This would be equivalent to having penny-farthings with driving wheels of about 2.5 metres and 0.75 metres! (Note that inches have been used in this example as they are still used in the cycle trade and by professional cyclists.)

Go-karts use a chain drive to the rear axle, as do motorbikes. If you have ever visited steam rallies, you may have noticed that the final drive to the driving wheels of steam lorries and cars is by a chain. Chains are used in preference to belts whenever accurate synchronisation of the angular speed of the two shafts is important, for belts often slip on pulleys. Thus in a car engine the camshaft which operates the opening and closing of the valves to the cylinders used to be linked to the engine's crankshaft by a chain drive. However, modern engines now use belts and pulleys with teeth for this purpose as they are quieter in operation.

Not only does the study of belt and chain transmission give insight into these particular mechanisms, it also involves spatial concepts, ratio, scale factor and the product of directed numbers in a meaningful context.

Observe all the examples of belt/chain drive you come across. Try to measure or estimate pulley sizes or numbers of teeth on the sprockets and the transmission factors involved. Also try to give a reason for the gearing.

Belts are to be found in domestic appliances such as spin dryers, washing machines, carpet sweepers and electric mowers. Cars and bikes are obvious examples. If you visit a farm or a fairground or a factory or a textile mill or a science museum you will be surprised how widely used this simple mechanism is. At agricultural shows or steam rallies you may well see a circular saw or a threshing machine invariably being driven by a belt. How about a treadle spinning wheel?

Exercise 1

1   Find the transmission factor $t(AB)$ for each of the pulley systems illustrated below where the numbers associated with the pulleys are their diameters in centimetres.

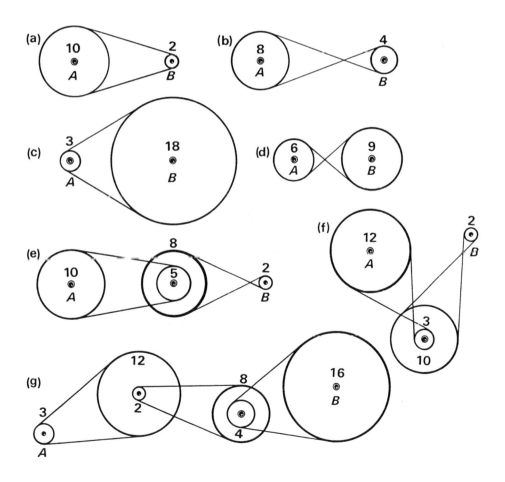

2   Meccano pulleys are available in the following sizes:
    12 mm, 24 mm, 36 mm, 48 mm, 72 mm and 144 mm.
        Show how they may be used to produce the
    transmission factors
    (a) +4   (b) −6   (c) +$\frac{1}{3}$ (d) −$\frac{2}{3}$ (e) +72

        Give other examples of transmission factors which
    can be produced using these pulleys and an example of
    at least one which is not possible.
        Which of the transmission factors +1, +2, . . ., +36
    could be produced using these pulleys? Could you
    achieve the same results with a smaller range of pulley
    sizes?

3   On most car engines a
    pulley on the crankshaft
    is connected by the 'fan
    belt' to the pulley which
    drives the fan and to the
    pulley which drives the
    alternator to keep the
    battery charged. The
    figure shows the
    arrangement for the
    engine of a typical family
    car. When the engine is
    turning at 3000 rpm at
    what speeds will the fan
    and the alternator be
    turning?

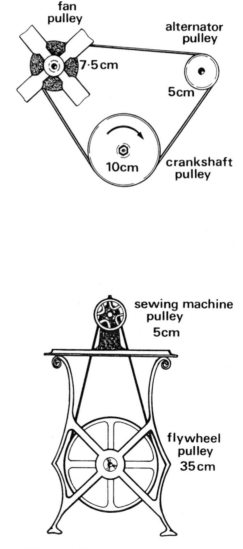

4   The large flywheel pulley
    on a treadle sewing
    machine is of 35 cm
    diameter and it drives a
    pulley on the sewing
    machine of 5 cm
    diameter. The sewing
    machine makes one stitch
    for each turn of its pulley.
    The flywheel is turned at
    one revolution per
    second. How many
    stitches will the sewing
    machine make in one
    minute?
        The sewing machine was 'modernised' by adding an
    electric motor on which was a pulley of diameter 1.25 cm

which was connected by a belt to the same 5 cm pulley on the machine. At what speed must the motor turn to drive the sewing machine at the same speed as before?

5   The main drum in an automatic washing machine is driven by a belt from an electric motor. The pulley on the motor has a diameter of 2 cm and that on the drum a diameter of 36 cm. At how many revolutions per minute is the drum rotating when the motor is turning at 3000 rpm?

6   The figure shows the system of chains and sprockets connecting the moving parts of a petrol engine grass mower. Find the transmission factor $t(AB)$ from the engine to the cutting blades, and $t(AC)$ from the engine to the roller. The roller has a diameter of 20 cm. At what speed will the engine be turning when the mower is moving at 1 metre per second? Assume no slipping and give the engine speed in rpm.

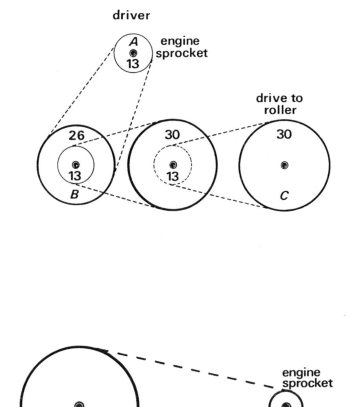

7   The rear axle carrying the driving wheels of a go-kart is connected to the engine by chain and sprockets. Different transmission factors are obtained by varying the number of teeth on the rear axle sprocket, to suit different racing circuits.

   One arrangement is shown above.

   What will be the speed of the rear axle when the engine is turning at 5120 rpm?

   What will the speed of the go-kart be if the road wheels have a diameter of 30 cm?

8   The following mechanisms were both observed in a 'country life' museum. The first consists of a pulley-cum-flywheel of 150 cm diameter, which would have been turned in the past by young apprentices. This was linked

13

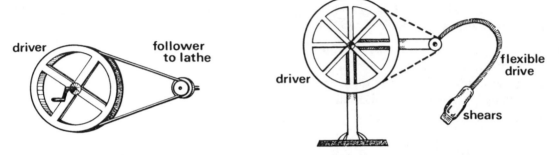

driver / follower to lathe / driver / flexible drive / shears

by a belt drive to a pulley block on a lathe, which had pulleys of diameters 10 cm and 25 cm. What are the possible transmission factors?

The second example is a piece of equipment used for shearing sheep. In this case the driver is a large sprocket with 192 teeth connected by a chain to a sprocket with only 8 teeth to give a high transmission factor. The output from the small sprockets was then conveyed by a flexible rotating shaft to a set of shears for cutting the woollen fleece off a sheep. If the driver is turned through 2 revolutions per second, what is the speed of rotation of the follower?

9 The gears on the Claude Butler Ladydale cycle are produced by chain wheels with 32 teeth and 50 teeth combined with 5 sprockets on the free wheel with 14, 17, 20, 24 and 28 teeth respectively. Complete the following table to give the 10 different transmission factors available. The gear of the cycle can then be determined in each case by multiplying the transmission factor by the diameter of the rear wheel, normally 27 inches.

| | | Number of teeth on free wheel | | | | |
		14	17	20	24	28
Number of teeth on chain wheel	32				1.33	
	50			2.50		

When José Meiffret broke the world speed record for a bicycle of just over 203 km/h he used a transmission factor of 10 between the chain wheel and free wheel so that its gear was equivalent to that of a penny-farthing with a wheel of about 7 m diameter. Suggest possible numbers of teeth for the chain wheel and free wheel. Why would it be difficult to produce a higher gear by this method?

14

11 A typical BMX bicycle
has 20 inch wheels, a
chain wheel with 36 teeth
and a free wheel with 18
teeth.
    What is its gear?
    What chain wheel and
free wheel would give
approximately the same
gear on a bicycle with
27 inch wheels?

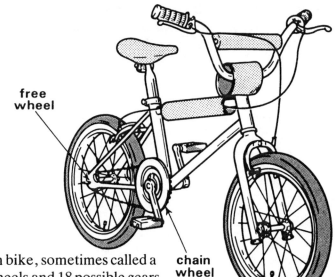

**free
wheel**

**chain
wheel**

12 The Dawes Wildcat all terrain bike, sometimes called a
mountain bike, has 26 inch wheels and 18 possible gears.
These are obtained by 3 sizes of chain wheel with 32,
40 and 48 teeth respectively, driving a free wheel with
6 sprockets having 16, 20, 24, 28, 32 and 36 teeth
respectively. Find all the possible gears and list them in
ascending order indicating how they are achieved.
Hence show how to move the chain to go through all
the gears in order starting with the lowest.

13 The hub ratios for the Sturmey–Archer FM hub gears
are:

first 0.666;   second 0.857;   third 1;   fourth 1.125.

What do these ratios mean?
    If the bicycle to which this hub is fitted has a 26 inch
wheel, a 42 teeth chain wheel and a 14 teeth sprocket,
find the cycle's gears.
    (NB A detailed reference on measuring the gear of a
bicycle can be found in *Even More Mathematical
Activities* by Brian Bolt, Activity 75.)

*14 The cross-section of the
cones for one half of a
variable gear system are
shown in the figure. What
is the range of pulley
diameters which can be
achieved by moving the
left hand cone towards or
away from the right hand
cone? What lateral
movement of the cone is
required to achieve the

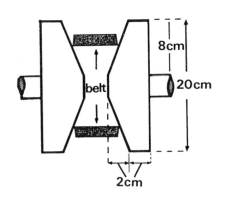

8cm

belt

20cm

2cm

15

full range of diameters? What range of transmission factors can be achieved between two shafts, connected by a belt over two of these 'variable diameter' pulleys?

*15 Find the length of the belt required for the pulley system below where the measurements are given in centimetres.

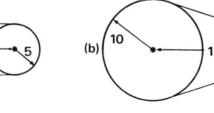

(a)

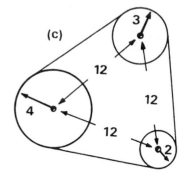

(b)

(c)

16 The efficient operation of a petrol engine depends on the precise timing of the opening and shutting of valves and the sparking of the spark plugs. This is co-ordinated by a belt connecting the engine's crankshaft to the camshaft and to a shaft which turns the rotor in the distributor. To ensure no slipping occurs, a tensioning pulley (the jockey wheel) is sprung to push against the belt to take up any slack. Try to find out why the camshaft pulley and ignition pulley are the same size, and twice the size of the crankshaft pulley, on most 4 cylinder car engines.

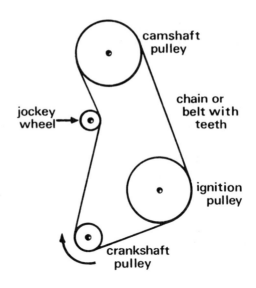

17 What are the advantages of (i) vee belts, (ii) toothed belts, over flat belts?

18 How is the waveband indicator on a radio linked to the tuning knob?

19 The stairs and the hand rail of an escalator are not unlike a chain and a belt. See what you can find out about their operation.

20 Conveyor belts are used for many industrial processes. Find examples of their use and analyse this use.

21 Why are flat belts often put onto pulleys in the form of a Möbius strip?

22 Sometimes a piece of machinery driven by a belt needs to be able to move to and fro while still keeping the belt taut. This can be achieved as shown below by the use of additional pulley wheels. In this mechanism it is required to drive pulley C from pulley A, but for the shaft which carries C to make significant movements to left and right. Pulley B is on a fixed shaft relative to A, while pulley D is on a shaft which moves with that of C. Explain carefully why the length of belt required remains the same as the carriage carrying C and D is moved sideways. What conditions must be satisfied concerning the diameters of the 4 pulleys and the relative positions of their shafts, for the movement of the carriage to be possible?

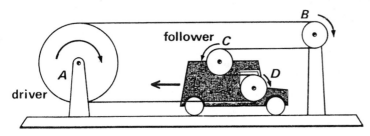

A good example of the use of this device is with the *mule* used in woollen mills for drawing and twisting yarn.

23 So far, all the examples of rotation considered have involved parallel shafts, but ways have been found of overcoming this both with belts and pulleys and with gear wheels.

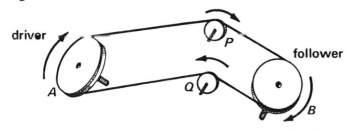

Using two jockey pulleys like P and Q above, a belt can be steered around corners to transmit motion between a driver A and follower B at almost any angle. If you are observant, you will see this in use to drive industrial machinery and agricultural machinery. Record any examples you find.

17

2 Gnashing teeth

An analysis of gear trains

The precision cut gears of
modern machines have come
a long way from the primitive
interlocking dowels and pegs
used in pre-Christian times
and still observable in old corn
mills today. Ancient Greeks
such as Hero in AD 60 were
very aware of the use of
intermeshing cogs and

described many uses of gear trains, while in the sixteenth
century, the genius Leonardo da Vinci was making elaborate
sketches showing that he was not only aware of gear trains,
but also of the importance of the shape of the teeth of a gear
wheel.

Gear wheels are rather like two cylindrical rollers with
projecting teeth which mesh with each other as the wheels
turn on their shafts, transmitting rotary motion from one to
the other. When two gears are meshed as shown below, the
follower always rotates in the opposite direction to the
driver, and with the number of teeth given

$$t(AB) = -2$$

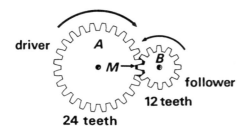

Gears are available in construction kits such as Meccano,
Lego and Fischertechnik (see the list of resources) to give
practical experience of what happens when gears mesh. But
they can also be understood by concentrating on the number
of teeth which pass the point M, where they mesh. When
the driver A, above, makes one clockwise revolution, 24
teeth pass downwards past M and pull 24 teeth of B the same
way, so B must make 2 anticlockwise turns. In general, when
two gears mesh

$$t(AB) = - \frac{\text{number of teeth on } A}{\text{number of teeth on } B}$$

18

Spur gears

When discussing gears it is helpful to use the correct terminology. When two or more gear wheels are meshed together, they are said to form a *gear train*. The commonest type of gear wheels are like the Meccano ones shown above, known as *spur gears*, and the smaller of two meshing gear wheels is generally termed the *pinion*. The larger of two meshing wheels is variously called the *wheel* or the *gear*.

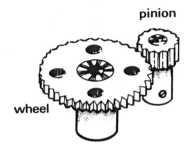

pinion

wheel

It is important to be able to calculate transmission factors for complex gear trains where several gear wheels are involved. In the figure below where numbers refer to teeth on the wheel,

$$t(AE) = t(AB) \times t(BC) \times t(CD) \times t(DE)$$

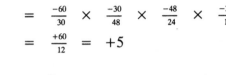

$$= \frac{-60}{30} \times \frac{-30}{48} \times \frac{-48}{24} \times \frac{-24}{12}$$

$$= \frac{+60}{12} = +5$$

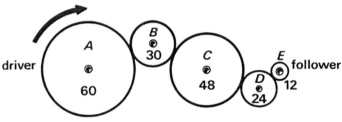

Notice how all the fractions cancel so that the *gear ratio* depends only on the number of teeth on the driver and on the follower. All that the intermediate wheels can do in a gear train of this kind is to determine the direction in which the follower turns relative to the driver, and thus the *sign* of the transmission factor.

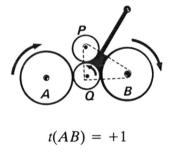

$$t(AB) = +1$$

One way of seeing why this is so is to realise that a single turn of the driver above is equivalent to moving all the gear wheels 60 teeth on, as each wheel transmits the same movement of teeth from one to another, and that adjacent wheels rotate in opposite directions.

A simple reversing mechanism on clockwork motors for toys was based on the idea of pulling a lever to introduce another gear wheel into the train as shown on the right. With *A* and *B* linked only by *Q*, the wheels *B* and *A* turn in the same direction, but a pull of the lever disengages *Q* from *A* and introduces *P* between *A* and *Q*, so reversing the direction of *B*. Note that the bracket holding *P* and *Q* pivots about the centre of *B*. Why must this be?

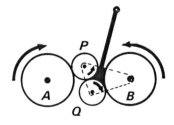

$$t(AB) = -1$$

19

To obtain very high or very low transmission factors without using very large wheels and small pinions, it is usual to mount two gear wheels on the same shaft as with pulley systems. In the gear train illustrated a transmission factor of +16 has been achieved as

$$t(AD) = t(AB) \times t(BC) \times t(CD)$$
$$= -4 \times +1 \times -4 = +16$$

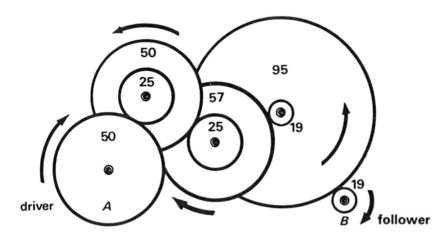

Without resorting to this approach, it would have required a driver with 16 times as many teeth as the follower, together with any conveniently sized gear wheel to link them, to ensure they turned in the same direction.

In practice, the actual gear wheels used to obtain a required transmission factor will depend on the standard gears available and the distances between the shafts to be driven. My Meccano set, for example, contains spur gears with 95, 57, 50, 25 and 19 teeth, but only some pairs can be meshed together because of the possible distances between the shafts. The possible pairings are:

50 and 25, giving a 2:1 ratio
57 and 19, giving a 3:1 ratio
95 and 19, giving a 5:1 ratio
95 and 25, giving a 19:5 ratio
95 and 27, giving a 5:3 ratio

Even with these restrictions, the gears can be combined to give a large range of transmission factors. The figure below shows how to achieve a transmission factor of +60 which would be necessary in the design of a traditional clock. Which

$t (AB) = +60$

20

shaft would be connected to the minute hand and which to the hour hand?

In many situations spur gears are used to reduce the speed of rotation of the output shaft compared to the driver. This is the case with a winch or electric drill or a food mixer. It is achieved by having spur wheels with a small number of teeth driving spur wheels with a large number of teeth. The gear train below is for a winch. The follower, which is

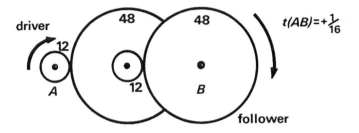

driver

48   48 $t(AB)=+\frac{1}{16}$

12

A   12   B

follower

connected directly to a winding drum, will turn at $\frac{1}{16}$ of the speed of the driver, so that a person turning a handle to operate A will gain a considerable mechanical advantage.

If $t(AB)$ is a high gear then $t(BA)$ is a low gear and more precisely

$$t(BA) = \frac{1}{t(AB)}$$

The gear box of a car, as its name suggests, depends on the ingenious use of gear trains to convey the rotary speed of the engine's crankshaft into different output speeds for varying driving conditions. To appreciate the workings of a gear box, consider the design of a 3-speed box as shown. The shaft carrying gear wheels B and C is not fixed to the drive shaft which carries gear wheel A, but is in line with it. In the position shown above the box is in *neutral*. Gear wheel A meshes with gear wheel D, and turns the shaft carrying gear wheels E, F and G, but they are not meshed with B or C so the follower does not turn.

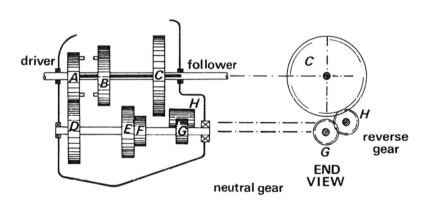

driver   follower   C

A   B   C   H

D   E F   G   H
reverse
gear

G

neutral gear   END
VIEW

The shaft carrying wheels *B* and *C* has a groove along its length and *keys* in these wheels slot into the groove. This allows the wheels *B* and *C* to slide along the shaft but ensures that they turn together with it.

First gear is obtained by sliding gear wheel *C* to the left to mesh with gear wheel *F*. This gives the transmission factor

$$t(AC) = t(AD) \times t(FC)$$

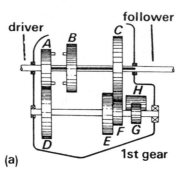
(a) 1st gear

Second gear is obtained by sliding gear wheel *B* to the right to mesh with gear wheel *E*. This gives the transmission factor

$$t(AB) = t(AD) \times t(EB)$$

Top gear is obtained by sliding gear wheel *B* to the left until the protruding lugs on its side engage with the lugs protruding from the side of wheel *A*. The effect is to lock *A* and *B* to turn together, giving a direct drive between the driver and follower.

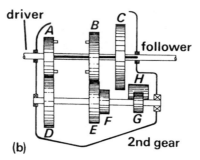
(b) 2nd gear

Reverse gear is obtained by sliding the reverse idler gear *H* to the left so that it meshes with gear wheel *C* while still meshing with gear wheel *G*. This gives the transmission factor

$$t(AC) = t(AD) \times t(DG) \times$$
$$t(GH) \times t(HC)$$

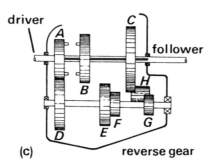
(c) reverse gear

In racing cars, the gears are chosen to suit a particular circuit. As the number of teeth of a given size is proportional to the circumference of a wheel and hence its diameter, it follows that in a gear box the total number of teeth on pairs of gear wheels such as *A* and *D*, *B* and *E*, and *C* and *F* must be the same. Replacing *A* and *D* by two wheels which give a higher ratio will influence all the gears except top gear, whereas *B* and *E* could be replaced and only change second gear. Further gears can be obtained by having a longer gear box and adding further pairs of gear wheels to the two shafts.

Transmitting rotary motion through an angle

Rotary motion is commonly transmitted between perpendicular shafts, and various types of gear wheels have been designed for this purpose, of which three are shown below.

bevel gears

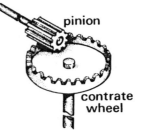
pinion

contrate wheel

Bevel gears are a fairly obvious adaptation of spur gears and are readily seen as the main mechanism in a hand drill.

With the Stanley drill below the driver A has 56 teeth and the follower B, which is directly linked to the drill chuck, has 15 teeth. The pulley X turns freely and is there to take some of the pressure off the main bearing of the driving wheel when drilling is taking place.

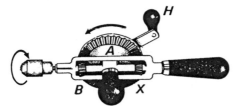

The efficiency of the drill depends on many factors such as the speed at which it is turned and the force which can be applied at the cutting edge of the drill bit. This last is related to the ratio of the distance moved by the handle H and the distance moved by the edge of the drill. With the above drill H travels on a circle of diameter 14 cm, so if it was turning a drill bit of diameter 0.5 cm then in one turn of the handle

H travels 14π cm

the edge of the drill travels $\frac{56}{15} \times 0.5\pi$ cm

giving a ratio of $14\pi : \frac{56}{15} \times 0.5\pi$

$$= 7.5 : 1$$

The hand turning the handle is thus moving 7.5 times as fast as the cutting edge of the drill bit, and if there was no friction in the drill mechanism it would mean that the force available at the cutting edge would be 7.5 times that applied to the handle. (See chapter 11 for an explanation based on the work done by a force.)

The mechanism for an egg whisk often uses a contrate wheel to mesh with pinions which drive the carefully synchronised rotors which do the whisking. Examination of one egg whisk showed 52 teeth on the contrate wheel and 11 teeth on the pinions, so that the rotors made almost 5 turns for each turn of the handle.

The worm gear is an ingenious invention, which can be seen, for example, in the mechanism used for tensioning a tennis net. It has only one tooth which travels around the gear in the form of a screw. It is used in conjunction with a spur gear and its effect is to move the spur gear forward one tooth for each complete revolution of the worm. The worm can only be used as a driver and always produces a low gear ratio. For example, if a worm gear is meshed with a spur wheel having 60 teeth then the worm gear must make 60 complete revolutions to produce one revolution in the spur gear. I used such a combination to reduce the very high speed of a small diesel engine to manageable proportions when making a model car. Even so, the car was capable of 65 km/h.

Practical activities

The availability of gears in the excellent construction kits such as Lego Technic, Fishertechnik and Meccano, makes practical work in constructing and experiencing gear trains a real possibility. Pupils can follow the work cards given in the kits or experiment on their own. In practice, most pupils like to be given straightforward tasks before they gain the confidence to invent their own gear trains. A motor too adds extra interest and motivation.

In addition to making up gear trains from work cards, pupils should be encouraged to observe gears in use in the world outside the classroom and to make a note of them. Sketches, photos and models of what has been observed are then worthwhile follow ups.

Visits to machine shops, textile mills, old flour mills and museums of various kinds will also generate more ideas.

Competitions to design a mechanism to lift the biggest weight or climb the steepest hill or whatever, will often stimulate groups to work in teams to come up with the ultimate design.

The *Power Game* is a commercially produced game where each player has the positioning of 8 gear wheels on a base board under their control and they have to try to use their moves to mesh these wheels with their opponent's wheels in a particular way. It is excellent for increasing spatial awareness of gear trains.

*Epicyclic gear trains

In all the gear trains considered so far, the gear wheels have turned about fixed shafts, but systems of gears known as epicyclic gears have been developed where gear wheels, known as planets, circle around a gear wheel with a fixed axis, known

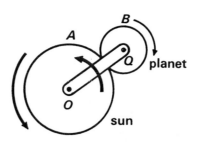

as the sun. This is the type of gear wheel used in 3 and 4 speed hub gears on a bicycle and in general they are used to produce large changes in speed using a small number of gear wheels. They are also the basis of the automatic gear boxes found in expensive cars.

To enable us to understand the gear ratios involved in epicyclic gear trains it is first necessary to understand the relationship between the tangential speed of a point P moving around a circle of radius r and its angular speed ω.

If θ is the angle at the centre subtended by an arc of length s then

$$s = r\theta$$

where θ is measured in radians. Differentiating this equation with respect to time gives

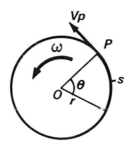

$$\frac{ds}{dt} = r\frac{d\theta}{dt}$$

But $\dfrac{ds}{dt}$ is equivalent to the tangential speed of P, V_P, and

$$\frac{d\theta}{dt} = \omega$$

so

$$V_p = r\omega \qquad (1)$$

Consider now the velocities of different points on the circumference of a wheel, of radius r, whose axis has a linear velocity V from left to right as well as an angular velocity of ω in a clockwise direction.

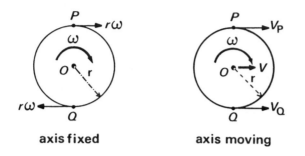

| axis fixed | axis moving |

If P is the point at the top of the wheel it would have a velocity of $r\omega$ from left to right if the axis were fixed. But the axis is moving in the same direction with speed V, so V_P, the actual velocity of P, will consist of the velocity of the axis together with the velocity of P relative to the axis:

$$V_P = V + r\omega \text{ from left to right.} \quad (2)$$

Similarly, the velocity of Q, the point at the bottom of the wheel, will be the sum of the velocity of the axis together with the velocity of Q relative to the axis. As the wheel is turning clockwise then Q is moving from right to left relative to the axis so

$$V_Q = V - r\omega \text{ from left to right.} \quad (3)$$

The velocities of other points can be obtained in a similar manner, but because the two velocities being added will be at an angle it will require the use of vector addition and as it is not required for our present analysis it will not be pursued here.

We are now in a position to analyse the basic epicyclic gear train.

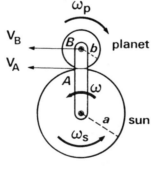

Let ω_S, ω_P and ω be the angular velocities of the sun gear, the planet gear, and the rod OB which determines the speed at which the planet orbits the sun. Let a and b be the radius of the sun and planet gears, and V_A and V_B the velocities of A, the point of contact of the two wheels, and of B, the axis of the planet wheel.

Then, as OB is rotating about O with angular velocity ω, using equation (1)

$$V_B = OB.\omega = (a + b)\omega \qquad (4)$$

Now as A can be considered as a point on the planet wheel which is turning clockwise with angular speed ω_P, from equation (2) its speed is given by

$$V_A = V_B + b\omega_P \qquad (5)$$

which, making use of (4) gives

$$V_A = (a + b)\omega + b\omega_P \qquad (6)$$

But if A is considered as a point on the sun wheel which is turning anticlockwise with angular speed ω_S, then using (1) again

$$V_A = a\omega_S \qquad (7)$$

Because gears don't slip these speeds must be equal, so

$$a\omega_S = (a + b)\omega + b\omega_P$$

$$\Rightarrow a(\omega_S - \omega) = b(\omega_P + \omega)$$

$$\Rightarrow \frac{\omega_P + \omega}{\omega_S - \omega} = \frac{a}{b}$$

But the number of teeth on the gear wheels is proportional to their radii, so

$$\boxed{\frac{\omega_P + \omega}{\omega_S - \omega} = \frac{t_S}{t_P}}$$

where t_S and t_P are the numbers of teeth on the sun and planet gears respectively.

Also note that although this relationship has been deduced measuring the angular speeds in radians per second (even though this was not made explicit), since they occur in the formula as a ratio we can measure the angular speeds in whatever units we like (e.g. revolutions per minute) as long as we are consistent.

As an example, consider the system where the sun gear has 24 teeth and the planet gear has 12 teeth. There are three special cases to consider.

Case (i)

The bar OB is fixed so that the planet gear does not orbit the sun. Then $\omega = 0$ and the formula gives

$$\frac{\omega_P + 0}{\omega_S - 0} = \frac{24}{12} \Rightarrow \omega_P = 2\omega_S$$

which is a result which could have been anticipated, for with OB fixed, the gears behave like normal spur gears.

Case (ii)

The sun gear does not rotate, then $\omega_S = 0$ and

$$\frac{\omega_P + \omega}{0 - \omega} = 2 \Rightarrow \omega_P = -3\omega$$

The negative sign here indicates that the planet wheel will be turning in the opposite direction to the arrow in the diagram, and hence in the same direction as OB is rotating.

Case (iii)

The planet gear does not rotate, then $\omega_P = 0$ and

$$\frac{0 + \omega}{\omega_S - \omega} = 2 \Rightarrow \omega_S = \tfrac{3}{2}\omega$$

The last two cases are not at all obvious or intuitive, but may be better appreciated by experimenting with rolling coins of different sizes about a fixed coin. Better still, make an actual model of an epicyclic gear using a suitable construction kit and investigate what happens as it is rotated. If, with the gear described, the sun is turned anticlockwise at 600 rpm, and the bar is rotated anticlockwise at 400 rpm, we can use the formula to find the speed of rotation of the planet wheel.

$$\frac{\omega_P + 400}{600 - 400} = \frac{24}{12}$$

$$\Rightarrow \omega_P + 400 = 400$$
$$\Rightarrow \qquad \omega = 0$$

An interesting and perhaps surprising result. It means that the planet wheel, although orbiting the sun, does not change direction. It always points the same way. If, on the other hand, the bar OB was rotated at 400 rpm clockwise, then

$$\omega = -400$$

giving

$$\frac{\omega_P - 400}{600 + 400} = 2$$

$$\Rightarrow \omega_P = 2400$$

a very different outcome!

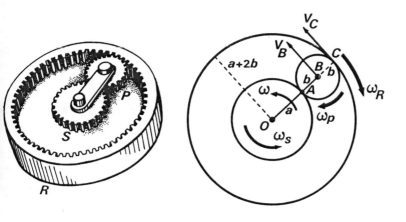

In practical applications of epicyclic gears, the planet gear P meshes with an annular ring gear R, and it is the relative speeds of the sun gear S, the rotating arm, and the annular gear R which are used. But how are they related? We can solve this very important relationship in kinematics using the same approach as with the simpler epicyclic gear train.

Let the sun and planet gear have radii a and b, then the outer ring gear will have radius $a + 2b$. Also, let the sun, planet and ring gears have angular speeds ω_S, ω_P and ω_R in the sense shown in the diagram, and let the bar OB which drives the planet gear have angular speed ω.

The point of contact, C, of the planet wheel with the ring gear, can be seen either as a point on the planet wheel or as a point on the ring. If its tangential speed is V_C then:

seen as a point on the ring, $V_C = -(a+2b)\,\omega_R$ (8)

seen as a point on the planet, $V_C = V_B - b\omega_P$

$$\Rightarrow V_C = (a + b)\omega - b\omega_P \quad (9)$$

from (8) and (9), $-(a+2b)\omega_R = (a + b)\omega - b\omega_P$ (10)

Writing $(a + b)$ as $(a + 2b) - b$ to correspond to the radii of the ring and planet gears, this equation can be rearranged as

$$(\omega_R + \omega)(a + 2b) = (\omega_P + \omega)b$$

leading to

$$\frac{\omega_R + \omega}{\omega_P + \omega} = \frac{b}{a + 2b} \qquad (11)$$

But if t_P and t_R are the numbers of teeth on the planet and outer ring gears, they are proportional to the radii of the wheels, so

$$\boxed{\frac{\omega_R + \omega}{\omega_P + \omega} = \frac{t_P}{t_R}}$$

Further, from our earlier analysis we know that

$$\frac{\omega_P + \omega}{\omega_S - \omega} = \frac{t_S}{t_P}$$

so

$$\frac{\omega_R + \omega}{\cancel{\omega_P + \omega}} \cdot \frac{\cancel{\omega_P + \omega}}{\omega_S - \omega} = \frac{\cancel{t_P}}{t_R} \cdot \frac{t_S}{\cancel{t_P}}$$

giving

$$\boxed{\frac{\omega_R + \omega}{\omega_S - \omega} = \frac{t_S}{t_R}}$$

which is essentially the same formula as the one involving sun and planet gears, but replacing the planet gear by the ring gear. In fact the same basic formula applies to all epicyclic gear trains.

Consider the use of the last formula obtained in analysing a gear train where the sun has 80 teeth, the planet has 40 teeth, and the outer ring gear has 160 teeth. In this train

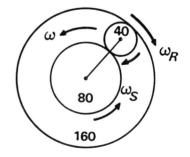

$$\frac{\omega_R + \omega}{\omega_S - \omega} = \frac{80}{160} = \frac{1}{2}$$

30

Suppose the sun is driven at 2400 rpm and that the outer ring gear is fixed so that $\omega_R = 0$. Then

$$\frac{0 + \omega}{2400 - \omega} = \frac{1}{2} \Rightarrow \omega = 800 \text{ rpm}$$

so the arm rotates anticlockwise at $\frac{1}{3}$ the speed of the input. If, instead of the ring gear being fixed, the arm was fixed so that $\omega = 0$,

$$\frac{\omega_R + 0}{2400 - 0} = \frac{1}{2} \Rightarrow \omega_R = 1200 \text{ rpm}$$

so the outer ring rotates clockwise at $\frac{1}{2}$ the speed of the input.
  Suppose now we fix the sun, and drive the arm at 2400 rpm. What happens to the outer ring gear?

$$\frac{\omega_R + 2400}{0 - 2400} = \frac{1}{2}$$

$$\Rightarrow \omega_R + 2400 = -1200 \Rightarrow \omega_R = -3600 \text{ rpm}$$

So the outer ring gear rotates anticlockwise at $1\frac{1}{2}$ times the speed of the arm.

*Rotation with a difference

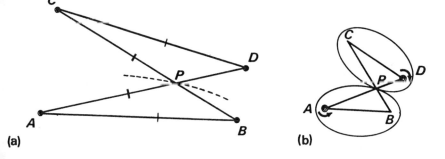

(a)   (b)

All the gear trains so far considered have been concerned with converting a constant speed input to a constant speed output, but mechanisms have been invented to produce variable transmission factors and two of these will now be considered.
  If a 4-bar linkage is made as shown above so that $AB = CD$ and $BC = AD$, then when it is crossed over it is always true that $AP + BP = $ constant, where P is the point of

31

intersection of AD and BC. This is easily seen from the symmetry of the figure which ensures that $BP = PD$ so $AP + BP = AP + PD = AD$, a fixed length. Now fix rod AB and as the linkage moves, the trace of P will be an ellipse with A and B as its foci. Similarly, if CD were fixed, P would trace out an ellipse with C and D as foci. Now imagine making two elliptical gear wheels equal in size to the ones traced out by P, and fixing them to bars AB and CD of the linkage. Let the elliptical gear on AB be fixed to a shaft at its focus A, and the elliptical gear of CD be fixed to a shaft at its focus D. The gears can then be rotated and the linkage ensures that they will always touch each other and have a common tangent at P.

In the position shown, if ellipse AB is the driver, its effective radius, AP, is larger than that of the follower, whose effective radius is DP. But the ratio of these radii is always changing, and varies from $\dfrac{e}{1-e}$ to $\dfrac{1-e}{e}$ and back again in the course of one revolution (where e is the eccentricity of the ellipses). Thus from a constant speed input, an output is achieved which is constantly varying in speed. The gear thus provides a slow feed and quick return mechanism which finds application in a number of machines.

The Geneva mechanism shown below gives an intermittent output from a constant speed input. It is used in ciné projectors and cameras where a frame is held still in front of the lens while being projected, before being rapidly moved on to make space for the next frame.

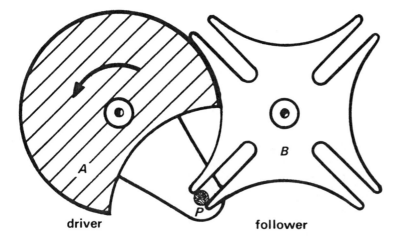

driver   follower

In the position shown, the raised pin P on the arm connected to the driver is about to enter one of the slots in the Maltese cross shape which forms the follower. As the driver rotates from the position shown, it turns the follower clockwise through 90°. This is only possible because of the portion cut out of the disc A which makes room for the prongs of B engaged by the pin. As soon as the cross has turned through 90° the pin P leaves its slot in the cross and the disc A engages with a curved portion of the cross preventing it from turning. The result is that for each turn of A, the Maltese cross is prevented from turning for $\frac{3}{4}$ of the turn and then flicked through 90° during the next $\frac{1}{4}$ of the turn.

Practical activities

If suitable tools are available, models can be made of the elliptical gears and of the Geneva mechanism. They can be made from plywood, preferably on a fairly large scale. The gears can be treated as rollers and the edges roughened by sticking on a strip of coarse sandpaper or the strips of foam used for draught-proofing. There is much satisfaction in making these models, and turning them is the best way to appreciate how they work. My own model of the Geneva mechanism never fails to fascinate young or old alike.

The Spirograph wheels do not have a central hole to allow their use as gear wheels in the normal sense but can be used to obtain some understanding of internal gears and epicyclic gears.

Exercise 2

1 The figure gives a variety of gear trains. The numbers indicate the number of teeth on the gear wheels. In each case, find the transmission factor $t(AB)$.

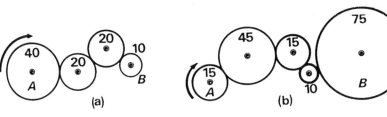

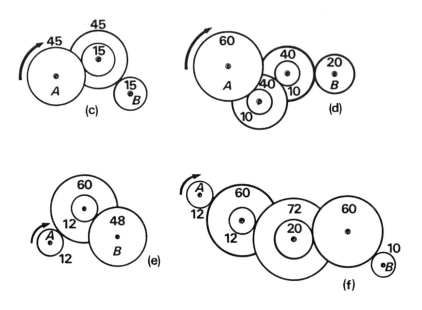

2 The Fischertechnik construction kit contains gears with
   10, 20, 30 and 40 teeth respectively. Show how these
   may be used to give gear trains with the following
   transmission factors:

   (a) −4   (b) +6   (c) +8   (d) −8
   (e) +3   (f) +24   (g) −$\frac{1}{2}$ (h) −$\frac{3}{2}$
   (i) −$\frac{1}{12}$ (j) +$\frac{3}{4}$

3 Find the transmission factors for the gear box described
   on page 21 when the gear wheels have the following
   numbers of teeth.

   A: 24, B: 40, C: 56, D: 48, E: 32, F: 16, G: 12, H: 12.

   How will they change if A has 27 teeth, and D has 45?
   Design a gear box in which the direct drive is not the
   highest gear.

4 The figure shows a 4-speed gear box. Gear wheel A on
   the drive shaft is always in mesh with gear wheel B on
   the layshaft on which are rigidly mounted gear wheels
   C, D and E. Gear wheels P, Q and R are all keyed to
   the follower shaft, so that they turn together but can be
   slid sideways along it to engage different gears on the
   lay shaft. Q and R are linked together so they cannot
   slide independently.

The gear box is shown in neutral. First gear is obtained by sliding R to the right to engage with E; second gear is obtained by sliding Q to the right to engage with D; third gear is obtained by sliding P to the right to engage with C; top gear is obtained by sliding P to the left so that it locks with A to give direct drive.

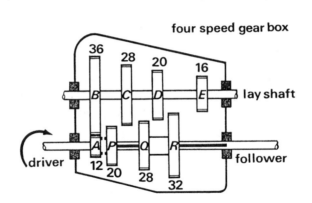

four speed gear box

Find the transmission factor for each gear and the speed of the follower shaft when the driver is rotating at 4000 rpm.

5 The gearing of a typical traditional mangle for squeezing water out of clothes is shown on the right. The flywheel is turned by hand and drives the bottom roller through a gear train consisting of 4 gears: A and C with 12 teeth, B and D with 32 teeth. The top roller is synchronised to turn at the same speed as the bottom roller, but in the opposite direction, by gears E and F which both have 16 teeth.

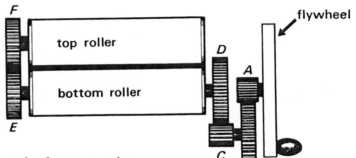

What is the transmission factor from the flywheel to (i) the bottom roller, (ii) the top roller?

6 In the past, the horse was the main source of power for many jobs, and the mechanism shown in the figure was invented to enable the horse's strength to be put to use in driving heavy machinery which required a rotary input. The horse was walked in a circle of approximately 2.5 metres radius, pulling an arm which rotated a large contrate wheel which had 72 teeth. This wheel engaged a pinion with 12 teeth which was linked by a universal coupling to a long drive shaft, which turned whatever piece of machinery required turning.

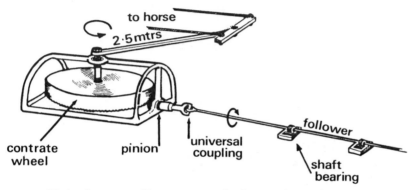

to horse

2·5mtrs

follower

contrate
wheel

pinion

universal
coupling

shaft
bearing

If the horse walks at a steady 2 m s^{-1} at what speed will the following shaft turn?

(NB The horse will need to step over the following shaft in the course of each circuit!)

7 A modification of the spur gear wheels is when one spur gear engages with the teeth on the inside of a ring, as shown on the right to form *internal gears*. As with spur gear wheels, the ratio depends on the numbers of teeth, but this time the ring and the pinion rotate in the same direction. This is the gear

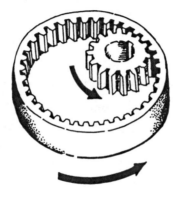

normally found in a hand lawn mower, where the driving wheels form the rings and the pinion is attached to the cutting blade shaft. In one well known make, the ring has 65 teeth and the pinion 13 teeth. There are 5 cutting blades on the rotor and the driving wheels have diameter 19 cm.

How many rotating cutting blades pass the fixed cutting blade for one revolution of the driving wheels? How far does the lawnmower move forward between one rotating cutting blade and the next meeting the fixed cutting blade?

8 In designing a gear train for a given purpose it is usual to use standard sizes of gear wheels. For efficiency, the smaller the number of wheels used the better. Design a gear train with a transmission factor of +315, from stock which includes gear wheels with tooth numbers from 12 to 88 in steps of 4.

9 The gear train shown on the right can be made using Meccano gears, to greatly reduce the speed of rotation of the driver and turn it through 90°. If the driver is being turned by an electric motor at 3000 rpm, what will be the speed of rotation of the follower?

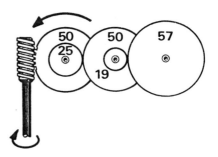

10 Lego Technic contains a good selection of gears, including spur wheels with 8, 16, 24 and 40 teeth and a worm gear. How could these be used to obtain:
(a) a transmission factor on parallel shafts of +60?
(b) a reduction ratio on perpendicular shafts of 1:240?

11 Design a 5-speed gear box where the transmission factors vary from $+\frac{1}{8}$ to +1.

12 Analyse
(a) the gears in a fishing rod.
(b) the mechanism in a cycle bell.
(c) the gear trains in a clock or watch.
(d) the gears of an egg whisk.
(e) the gears of a hand drill.
(f) the gears of an electric drill.
(g) the gears of a lathe.
(h) the gears of a winch (often seen on fishing boats).
(i) the gears of an old-fashioned mangle.
(j) the gears in a flour mill.
(k) the gears driving a cycle speedometer.
*(l) hub gears on a cycle.
(m) the gears in a lawnmower.
(n) the gears in a musical box.
(o) the gears in a clockwork or friction toy.

13 Toys powered by an electric motor are usually low geared, for the motor will normally rotate at a higher speed than is required for the output shaft. See what you can find.

14 Why does the driver of a traction engine or steam roller have to turn the steering wheel through many complete turns to go around a sharp bend? Examine the steering mechanism on such an engine if you get an opportunity to go to a steam rally.

15 Investigate the gears used in the mechanism used for tensioning the wire on which a tennis net is suspended. By how much does each turn of the handle shorten the wire?

*16 A simple epicyclic gear train has 36 teeth on the sun gear and 24 teeth on the planet gear. Find the speed of rotation of the planet gear when the sun gear is driven at 3000 rpm and

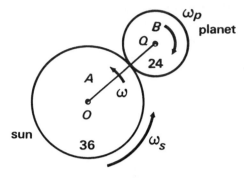

(a) the arm OQ is stationary
(b) the arm OQ is rotating at 1000 rpm.

*17 An epicyclic gear train consists of a sun gear S with 40 teeth surrounded by three planet gears P_1, P_2 and P_3 each having 40 teeth and connected to each other by a ring R. Outside the planet gears is an annular gear A with 120 teeth.

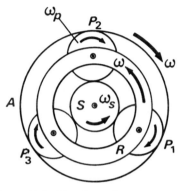

(a) Find the speed of rotation of A, (i) when S rotates at 600 rpm and R is stationary, (ii) when R rotates at 600 rpm and S is stationary.
(b) What is the speed of rotation of R when $\omega_P = 0$ and S rotates at 600 rpm?
(c) What is the speed of rotation of S when R is rotating at 600 rpm and A at 200 rpm?

*18 The sun gear of an epicyclic gear train has 12 teeth and the outer annular gear C is fixed. How many teeth must the planet gear B and the annular gear C have if A is to turn 12 times as fast as the arm connected to the planet gear?

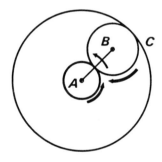

*19 In the epicyclic gear train shown, the planet gear B has k times as many teeth as the sun gear A.
Prove that the angular speeds of the sun, the arm

connecting the planet and the annular gear C satisfy the relation:

$$\frac{\omega_C + \omega}{\omega_A - \omega} = \frac{1}{1 + 2k}$$

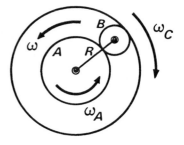

Hence show that

(a) when the arm is fixed $\qquad\qquad \omega_A = (1 + 2k)\omega_C$

(b) when the annular gear is fixed $\quad \omega_A = (2 + 2k)\omega$

(c) when the sun gear is fixed $\qquad \omega_C = \dfrac{-(2 + 2k)\omega}{1 + 2k}$

*20 Make use of the formula established in question 17 to investigate the transmission factors available from an epicyclic gear train when $k = 1$, $k = 2$, $k = \frac{1}{2}$.
  Why are there 6 transmission factors possible in each case from the one mechanism?
  What is the range of transmission factors from the rotating arm to the annular gear?

*21 The curved shape of a spur gear is cut in the shape of an involute (see figure). What are involutes and why are they used?

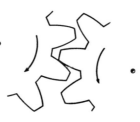

*22 When a car is driven around a bend, the outside wheels travel further than the inside wheels. Because of this, the wheels cannot be connected to the same shaft. They are driven separately through a specialised mechanism known as a *differential gear*. See what you can find out about the working and application of differential gears.

23 Rotary motion is frequently transmitted between two shafts at an angle using *universal joints*. Investigate the following:
(a) flexible couplings;
(b) Hooke's universal joint;
(c) a ball and socket universal joint;
(d) a constant velocity joint.
  Find where they are used and their limitations.

3 Tipping, tilting and turning

The variable-based triangle

The essential property of a triangle is its rigidity and this is exploited time and time again in static structures such as the timber framework of a roof. Much of traditional geometry and trigonometry has been about the properties of triangles and the relationships between their sides and angles, but always seen as static figures.

However an observant individual will also notice how the designer and engineer have made much use of triangle structures where one side of the triangle can vary in length. In the figure below the triangle ABC is made of 3 bars in such a way that the length of AB can be changed. As the length of AB is changed, one effect is to change the angles of the triangle such as θ while another is to change the distance, h, of C from AB.

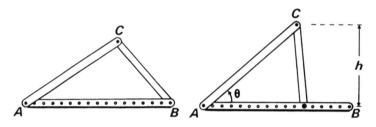

The example of such a mechanism seen in almost every home is the window fastening, where the bar holding the window open at a fixed angle has numerous holes in it, allowing it to be attached at different positions to a pin in the window frame. As the length of the bar varies, the window opens at different angles. A similar mechanism allows the desk top in a drawing office to be set at different angles, or the top of a garden frame to be opened to a different degree. Next time you lounge in a deck chair have a close look at the way it can be adjusted into different positions.

In these examples the variable side of the triangle can have its length changed in a number of discrete steps, usually equal. Does this lead to equal changes in the angle the window is opened or the desk top raised?

It is a good idea to carry out some practical experiments here using plastic geostrips, or Meccano strips, or strips of card joined by paper fasteners, to investigate how the angles of a triangle change with the change in length of one side. Theoretically of course this can be analysed using the cosine rule, but it is my conviction that this mechanism is not fully appreciated until some kind of model of it has been made and the way the angles change as AB changes length has been experienced.

What influence does the ratio of the fixed lengths of AC and AB have on the situation?

The examples of this mechanism considered so far have envisaged the length of AB changing in discrete steps, but other applications involve a screw which allows the length AB to be changed continuously. The two car jacks shown below are examples of this. Although these jacks look quite different, they behave in just the same way. Jack (a) can be seen as a 4-bar linkage in the form of a rhombus, with the diagonal AB consisting of a screw which changes the length of AB as it is turned. Because the resulting two triangles are isosceles, C and D will always lie on the perpendicular bisector of AB. In this use of the mechanism, it is the way in which the length of CD changes as AB changes which is important, not the change in the angles of the triangles. It is instructive to make a model of a rhombic linkage and, by measuring, find enough data to plot a graph of CD against AB. Better still, if a real jack of this type can be obtained, the height of C can be plotted against the number of turns of the screw AB. To start with, the jack rises quickly, but the rate of change slows as the jack gets higher. This is a useful feature of such a design, for it means the jack becomes lower geared as the load increases.

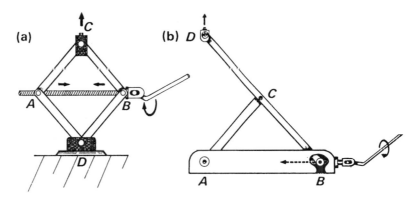

A simple model can be made of jack (b) using geostrips or card strips on a background card as shown. In the design of the jack $AC=BC=DC$ and this ensures that D moves in a straight line perpendicular to AB. In this form it is known as the Scott–Russell (or isosceles) straight line linkage because of this property, a feature which is clearly important. To see what happens when the lengths are not equal, trace the path of a point such as P and extend the length of DC to see what happens to D if $DC > BC$. An A-level candidate should be able to show that when $DC=BC$ the path of P is part of an ellipse.

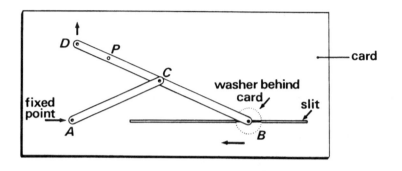

This jack is commonly used as the mobile jack mounted on wheels in motor garages or, upside down, as the stabilising mechanism on the corner of a caravan.

As with most if not all mechanisms, the variable-based triangle has *one degree of freedom*. By this is meant that once the movement of any one part of the mechanism is known, the movement of all the other parts is determined. Also, like other mechanisms, different parts serve the role of *driver* and *follower*. In the examples so far considered the input has been to change the length of AB, but the output has been variously: the angle at C for the window, the angle at A for the desk top, the distance of C from AB for the car jacks.

With a car foot-pump however the *driver* is rod AC which is turned to decrease angle C and in so doing forces the piston along the cylinder of the pump.

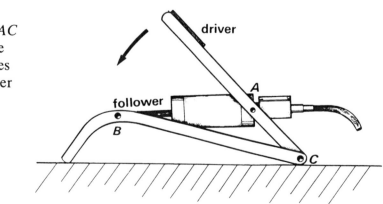

The independent suspension for a car wheel, or the suspension for the rear wheel of a motorcycle, often incorporates this mechanism where the main ingredient of the variable side of the triangle is a coiled spring.

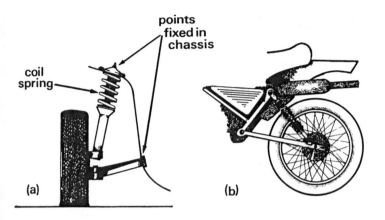

(a)　(b)

Hydraulic rams

Many machines have been revolutionised in the last 30 years by the introduction of a hydraulic ram as the variable side. The ram consists of a piston inside a cylinder filled with oil. The power from an engine is used to pump the oil from one side of the piston to the other, thus pushing the piston along the cylinder to shorten or lengthen the

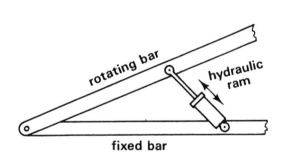

hydraulic ram, and in so doing changing the angle between AC and BC.

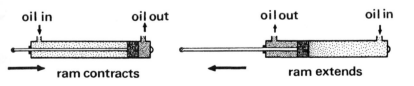

One of the simplest applications of this is seen in a lorry's tipping mechanism or, for example, the mechanism on skip transporters which is used to load or off-load the skips from the transporter.

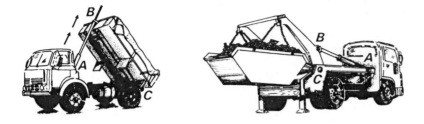

With the tipping mechanism the deck of the lorry has to be turned through about 60°, but with the skip transporter the lifting arm has to be turned through an angle of more than 90°. These differences are achieved by having rams of different lengths and varying the lengths of the fixed sides of the triangle, namely AC and BC.

Why is the maximum length of a ram AB always less than twice its minimum length?

On most large civil engineering or building contracts, whether for new roads, or dams, or dredging canals, or digging foundations, you are sure to see the modern excavators whose multiple-jointed jibs are like human arms on a large scale. These pieces of engineering equipment, like the one illustrated below, were originally made by JCB, but are now also made by other manufacturers such as Komatsu, and have proved their worth wherever trenches have to be dug or earth moved.

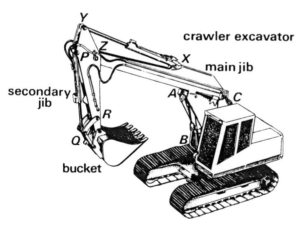

In the excavator illustrated there are 3 variable-based triangle mechanisms shown, all operated by hydraulic rams:

ABC alters the angle of the main jib, pivoting it in a vertical plane about C;

XYZ alters the angle of the secondary jib relative to the main jib, by rotating it about Z;

PQR alters the angle of the bucket relative to the secondary jib via a 4-bar linkage.

44

All these mechanisms can be operated independently by the driver of the excavator, enabling the bucket to reach and dig out earth in a wide range of positions. Once the fixed dimensions of the triangles and the range of lengths of the rams are known, then the full versatility of the excavator can be investigated.

The same hydraulic mechanism is used in many robots and also in automatic vents for greenhouses, where it is the change in pressure of a gas inside a cylinder which pushes the piston as the temperature rises.

Practical experiments can be carried out, and models made using the usual construction kits: Meccano, Fischertechnik, and Lego. The latter now has a pneumatics kit which enables the simulation of mechanisms using a pneumatic ram. Also, Technology Teaching Systems Ltd have produced a miniature pneumatics kit. But much can be achieved using card and paper fasteners without going to great expense.

Manufacturers of civil engineering equipment produce glossy advertising materials which are quite instructive, while engineering magazines are an excellent source of many applications.

Take special notice when next you see a mechanical digger, or crane, or tractor at work, or visit a fairground.

Exercise 3

1 Make a variable-based triangle using a construction kit or cardboard strips and paper fasteners. Change x the length of AB and measure the value of θ for each value of x you use.

   Plot a graph of θ against x

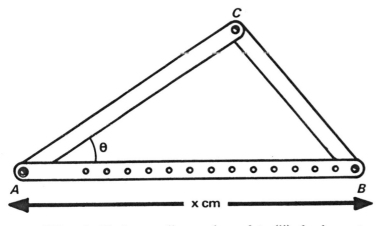

   What is (i) the smallest value of θ, (ii) the largest value of θ?

   Does θ change in equal amounts for equal changes in x?

2   A variable-based triangle has $AC=8$ cm, $CB=6$ cm and
    AB can take values of 3 cm, 4 cm, 5 cm, 6 cm, 7 cm,
    8 cm, 9 cm, 10 cm.
        What are the corresponding values of θ?
        What are the corresponding heights of C above AB?

3   A mechanism is to be
    designed to fix a desk top
    at angles of $15°, 30°, 45°$,
    and $60°$ to the horizontal.
    Suggest how it may be
    achieved, giving detailed
    measurements.

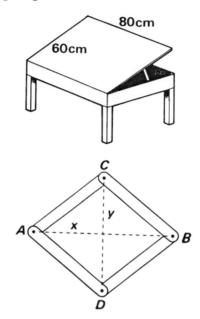

4   Make a rhombic linkage
    $ABCD$ and measure the
    corresponding values of
    the diagonals x and y for
    different positions of the
    linkage. Plot y against x.
        Can you explain why
    the graph will be part of
    a circle if equal scales are
    used on the axes?

5   As for question 4, but using a linkage in the form of a
    kite, draw a graph to show how the lengths of its
    diagonals are related.

6   A mechanism is made from two strips AC and BD as
    shown below, such that $AC=BC$. Fix A by using a
    drawing pin into a drawing board, or paper fastener into
    a large piece of card or paper. Draw a straight line across
    the paper through A and then trace the locus of different
    points P of DB as B moves along the line. Why is the
    locus of C a circle?

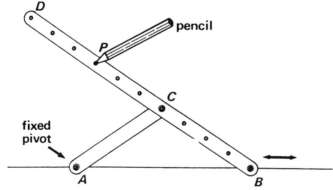

        Allow C to make a complete circle about A while
    keeping B on the line, to obtain the true paths of points
    like P.

7   An ironing board is to be
made to be adjustable
with working heights of
60 cm, 65 cm, 70 cm,
75 cm, and 80 cm. If the
legs are all of length
100 cm how can this be
achieved?

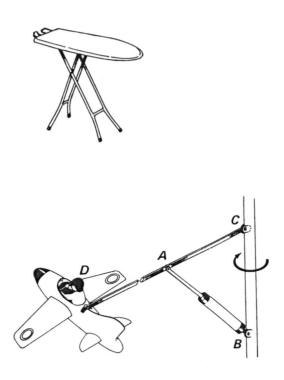

8   A children's fairground
ride consists of 8 small
planes, each attached to
a central rotating shaft by
a long arm such as CD
(see figure) and kept up
at an angle by a hydraulic
ram. As the shaft rotates,
the pilots in the planes
can operate controls
which extend and
contract the hydraulic
ram AB and make their
planes climb or dive at
will.

  Given that $CD=4$ m, $CA=1.5$ m, $BC=1.5$ m, and
AB can vary between 1.5 m and 2.5 m, find the possible
variation in the angle ACB by scale drawing or
trigonometry and hence find the variation in height of
a plane.

  What is the length of the ram when DC is horizontal?

  If the ride is designed for the planes to have a
maximum speed of 11 m/s (about 40 km/h) what is the
maximum angular velocity of the rotating shaft in
revolutions per minute?

9   A clothes airer is
designed as shown on the
right, where the
supporting framework is
rather like a trellis-work
fence. The total height of
the airer, and the spacing
between the rungs which
hold the clothes, is
determined by the
variable-based triangle
ABC.

Give realistic measurements for the lengths of the framework, and the two positions of B which will allow the airer to be erected so that the rungs are 28 cm or 36 cm apart vertically.

10   An automatic window opener is designed as shown below. AC is fixed to the window frame and W is attached to the window. As the temperature rises the increase in pressure of the gas in cylinder AD pushes the piston rod BA along the cylinder, and in so doing increases angle θ. Given that AC=24 cm, CB=12 cm, and that the gas cylinder AB can change in length from 18 cm to 33 cm, find the maximum change in the angle θ.

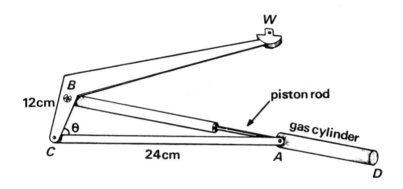

Further, given that CW=24 cm, find the distance between the extreme positions of W.

11   A large mobile crane, as shown below, can change the angle of its jib from horizontal to 80° using a pair of hydraulic rams AB, one each side of the jib. If the shortest length of the rams is 2 m, and AC=BC=2 m, to what length must the ram AB extend, and at what angle is BC to the horizontal?

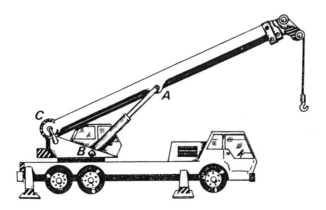

12 A derrick CA on a ship is
being raised by being
rotated about its end C
using a winch which winds
in the rope AB at a speed
of 1 metre every 5
seconds. If CA and CB
are of length 10 m how
long does it take to haul
the derrick from the
horizontal to the vertical?

Draw a graph to show
how θ, the angle of
elevation of the derrick,
changes with time.

How does the height of A change with time?
(*Hint.* Consider the change in length of AB at 10 second
intervals.)

13 A loft ladder is designed to lie flat on the loft floor when
not in use, but to be pulled down through a trapdoor
when needed. The mechanism used for this is shown.
$AC=70$ cm, $BC=75$ cm, and $AD=44$ cm. The points B
and C are fixed and the rod AC joins the ladder to C.
A small pulley wheel at B engages in a slot which runs
the length of the ladder, enabling the ladder to slide
along it.

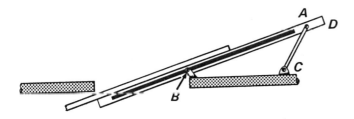

What is the locus of A as the ladder is moved?

How far (approximately) is D from B when the ladder
is lying flat?

If, when the ladder is in use, $AB=10$ cm, at what
angle is the ladder to the vertical? You may assume that
BC is horizontal. Given that each section of the ladder
is of length 2 m, and that when in use they overlap by
26 cm, how far is the floor beneath B?

49

Make a model or scale drawing of the ladder in different positions, to find the locus of *D* and hence the headroom needed above the loft floor for it to operate.

14 An up-and-over garage door is designed as shown using a variable-based triangle mechanism *ABC*. The door *XY* is 2 m high and *AC=CY=BC*=0.5 m. The door is opened from the outside by pulling *X* outwards and upwards. A projecting pin in the door at *A* slides in a vertical channel in the door post, while *C* is made to rotate about *B* by rod *BC*.

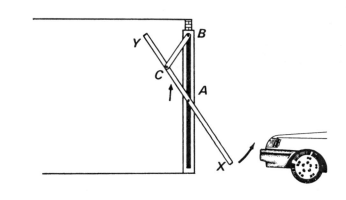

When the garage door is at 30° to the horizontal, how high will *X* be and how high will *Y* be?

How far from the garage door should the driver stop the car to be able to open the door?

What is the locus of *Y*?

15 When you flush a lavatory by turning a handle, the underlying mechanism is based on a triangle with one side consisting of a piston in a cylinder. Investigate the relationship between the angle through which the handle is turned and the lengths of the components of the mechanism to give the required movement of the piston in the cylinder.

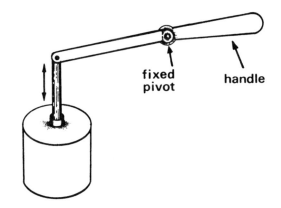

50

16 The piston rod of a steam engine is connected by the connecting rod *BC* to a flywheel which rotates about a fixed axis through *A*. *B* is constrained to move in a straight line through *A*. How is the *throw* of the piston (that is the distance between the extreme points of its motion) related to the lengths *AC* and *BC*?

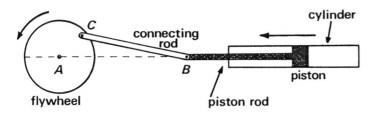

17 The vertical reciprocating motion of the needle of a sewing machine uses the variable-based triangle mechanism. *C* makes complete revolutions about *A* while *B* is constrained to move along a straight line by a guide.

How do the lengths of (i) *AC* and (ii) *BC* determine the movement of the needle?

Measure the total vertical displacement of the needle of a sewing machine and suggest lengths for *AC* and *BC* to give the same effect.

What additional mechanism is required to give a *swing needle* movement in addition to the vertical oscillations?

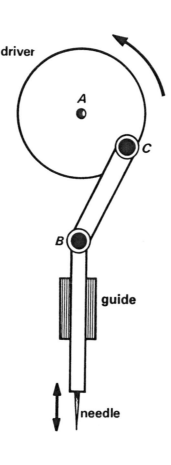

18 The range of movement which can be achieved using a hydraulic ram as the driver in a variable-based triangle is well illustrated by the specification for a JCB excavator in the following figure. The positions of the three rams operating the arms and the bucket are shown by arrows.

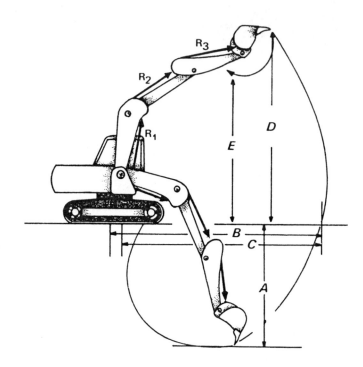

By considering the various configurations the arm and bucket can take, find the maximum and minimum length of the hydraulic rams involved.

How could the bucket and arms be manipulated to dig a level trench 1 m deep?

Excavator performance

A Dig depth

3.10 m

B Max reach G.L. from Slew Centre

4.75 m

C Max reach from King Post

4.22 m

D Max working height

3.60 m

E Max load-over height

2.5 m

Total Boom swing

100°

Bucket rotation angle

177°

19 The mechanism shown below, known technically as an oscillating crank mechanism, is driven by a constant speed motor which rotates the flywheel about C. A pin B on the flywheel engages in a slot in the bar AD which can rotate about the fixed point A. As the flywheel rotates, the pin B forces AD to oscillate about A in such a way that the time taken to go from right to left is longer than the time taken to go from left to right. The reason for this is shown in the right hand diagram. If angle B_2CB_1 is 60°, for example, then D will be moving from right to left for the time B takes to go from B_1 through 300° about C to B_2, and from left to right while B goes the 60° from B_2 to B_1. In this case the motion takes 5 times as long moving to the left as the motion to the right.

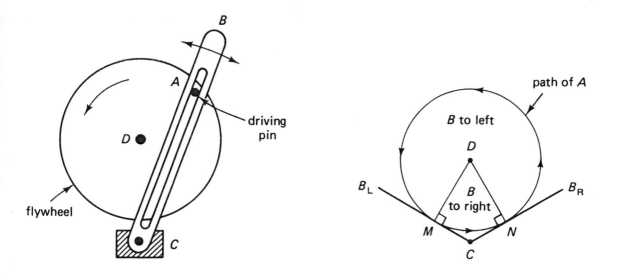

This mechanism is made use of in a joiners' shop where D is attached to a cutting blade which does work in one direction, as in planing wood, and then returns quickly. A slow feed and quick return.
(a) Give possible dimensions for AC and BC for angle B_2CB_1 to be 60°.
(b) When $AC=20$ cm and $BC=14$ cm find angle B_2CB_1 and the approximate ratio for the feed time to the return time.
(c) Given that $AC=20$ cm and it is required to fix the length of BC to obtain a ratio of feed time to return time of 8:1, find the length of BC to 3 significant figures.
(d) What happens if $BC>AC$?

20 The mechanism shown
on the right for a work-
table drive is a refinement
of the mechanism in the
previous question. It is
also used to give a slow
feed and quick return,
but whereas the previous
mechanism gave a very
variable speed, this
combination of two
variable-based triangle
mechanisms *ABC* and
DEA gives an almost
constant feed speed to
the follower *DF* when *BC*
is driven at a constant
angular speed.

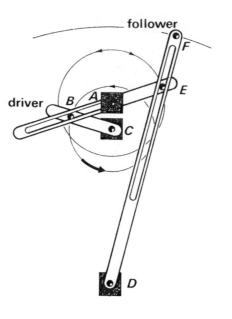

(a) Try making a model of this mechanism using card
strips and paper fasteners. In this case it will be
necessary to have *BC* above *AE* to allow *BC* to
make complete rotations.

(b) Find the angle turned through by *DF* when moving
from right to left for equal changes in the angle
turned by *BC*, either by using your model, or by
scale drawing. A suitable set of dimensions is:

AC=5 cm,
BC=8 cm,
AE=10 cm and
CD=25 cm.

21 Toggle clamps are used
industrially for clamping
something into position
with a large force. One
way of achieving this is to
use the mechanism
shown. As the angles at
A and *B* become small it
requires a large
movement of the handle
at *C* to produce a
relatively small
movement of the toggle
bolt *BD*. The force along
the length of *BD* is
roughly inversely
proportional to the ratio

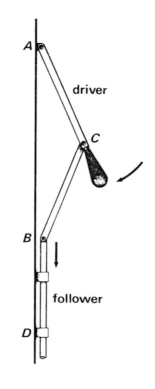

of the distance moved by BD compared to that of C, hence it is possible to produce a large force at D compared to that applied to C.

Given that $AC=BC=10$ cm plot a graph to show the length of AB compared to the distance of C from AB.

22 Measure the dimensions of a skip and try to design a skip transporter mechanism to load and off-load it successfully. Some skip transporters manage to carry two skips, one behind the other. Design a suitable mechanism to achieve this.

23 Good pruning shears are designed to give a sliding action as well as a cutting action. The design shown below makes use of a variable-based triangle mechanism. Try making a model of it using thick card and paper fasteners to see how the mechanism produces the required effect.

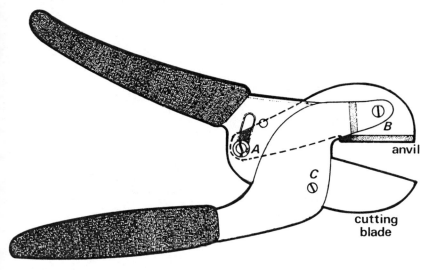

24 Keep an eye open for uses of the variable-based mechanism. Make a sketch or model of what you observe and try to decide which part is the driver and which the follower. Some examples you can look for are:

(a) umbrella mechanisms;
(b) base of a music stand, or slide projector stand;
(c) mechanisms for shop awnings;
(d) rotating clothes line;
(e) folding chairs;
(f) adjustable sights on a rifle;
(g) window opening mechanisms;
(h) cranes;
(i) undercarriage of a plane;
(j) civil engineering equipment.

25 In many garages the engine oil is stored in drums which have a pump mechanism attached as shown in the figure. This differs from the basic slider–crank mechanism in that the piston moves up and down in a line which is not through the pivots A and B.

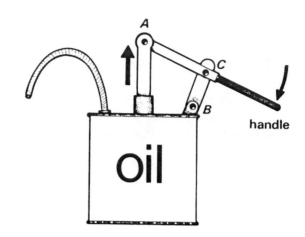

handle

Investigate such a modification, by the use of models, to see how the range of angles through which AC and BC turn, for a given movement of the piston, differs with the distance of B from the line of the piston.

26 Design a log grab, as shown, given that the hydraulic ram to be used can vary in length between 30 cm and 20 cm and the points of the grab are to be able to open to 80 cm.

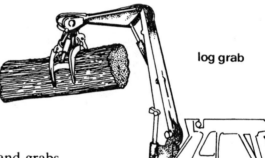

log grab

27 Investigate the Hyab hydraulic arms and grabs permanently attached to lorries which regularly carry heavy loads such as building bricks and timber.

28 Farm tractors are equipped with hydraulic mechanisms for manipulating the implements which they tow such as ploughs. See if you can examine their use and analyse how they operate. An agricultural show is an ideal place to see these.

4 Swings, lifts and balances

Applications of the parallelogram linkage

When four bars are pinned together at their ends to form a quadrilateral, they form what is known as a 4-bar linkage, and its use as a mechanism, often heavily disguised, is widespread. It has the feature that if one bar is held still and another is moved, then the movement of the remaining bars is precisely determined. Imagine fixing AB in the linkage shown and turning CB clockwise about B. CD will then turn AD clockwise about A. Can you see why CD will itself be rotating in an anticlockwise direction?

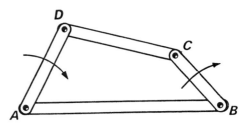

Before proceeding much further, it is a good idea to have some materials available for constructing linkages, such as Meccano, geostrips, or last, but by no means least, card strips and paper fasteners.

Make some 4-bar linkages and verify that when one bar is fixed the movement of the three remaining bars is determined by the movement of any one of them. This property ensures that the linkage has *one degree of freedom* and hence is very suitable as a mechanism. In contrast, construct a 3-bar linkage which does not allow any movement, and a 5-bar linkage where the movement of two bars would need to be known before that of the others was determined.

Parallelogram linkages

The simplest form of a 4-bar linkage is the one in which opposite bars are of equal length so that the linkage forms a parallelogram. Good examples of the use of this linkage are shown on page 58 with the sewing box, swing, and windscreen wipers. An analysis of its use shows that its significant function is to ensure that certain components always move parallel to each other.

The drawers of the sewing box form opposite bars of a parallelogram linkage, so that when they are opened they do not tip up, but stay horizontal. The large plank of the swing always stays level with the ground, in contrast to the motion of the swing boats in a fairground. But at the same time each point of the plank travels on an arc of a circle like a conventional swing. Why?

The letter balance or chemical balance or traditional kitchen balances all employ the parallelogram linkage to ensure that the scale pans stay horizontal as the beam of the balance tips.

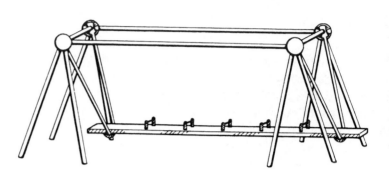

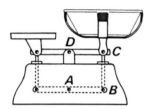

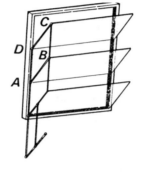

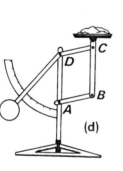

(d)

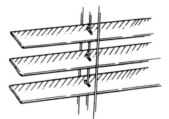

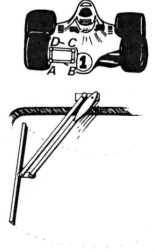

The car suspension on a grand prix car is designed to keep the very wide tyres flat on the road and is achieved by a parallelogram linkage which only allows the wheels to move vertically.

Another familiar use is the mechanism for the windscreen wipers on many buses, lorries and trains, which keeps the wiper blade vertical as it sweeps to and fro across the screen. It is interesting to contemplate in what ways the behaviour of such a windscreen wiper differs from the behaviour of traditional wipers on a car.

Sometimes the parallelogram linkage is used in a long thin form to operate on a distant object such as in a tree pruner or apple picker, or stunt kites where the long sides are the strings, and the kite and operator's body form the short sides.

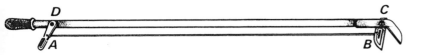

The connecting rods which link the driving wheels of steam locomotives, so that the wheels all turn together, form the fourth side of a parallelogram whose vertices are the wheel axles and the points of connection of the connecting shaft with the wheels. In this case D and C make complete revolutions about A and B unlike in the previous applications where the range of movement was constricted.

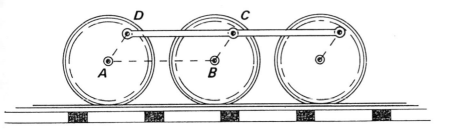

Pop-up books depend on parallelograms. As the book is opened, the various objects which are to stand up are pulled up by paper or card parallelograms, so that they always move parallel to the page being raised and lie flat when it is closed.

Have you ever wondered why maintenance engineers do not fall out of their 'buckets' when they lean over to see to the street lights? The arms of the elevator are raised using hydraulic rams, but the mechanism which keeps the bucket always at the same angle is a pair of parallelogram linkages.

No matter what angle the arms are at, the parallelograms ensure that QY is parallel to PX and SZ is parallel to RY. Now RY is kept vertical by being fixed at the appropriate constant angle to QY and so SZ is always vertical.

An identical mechanism is used to attach a straightedge to a draughtsman's drawing board so that the straightedge can be moved around the board, without turning, to draw parallel lines.

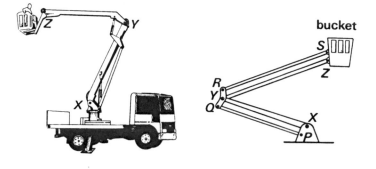

A very significant use of 4-bar linkages is to be found on modern excavators such as the JCB mechanisms on the bucket arm shown below. As the bucket arm is raised by turning about D, the angle of the bucket to the horizontal stays the same so that any material in it does not fall out. This is achieved by the parallelogram linkage $ABCD$ which ensures that the bar BCG always remains parallel to AD which is fixed in the framework of the excavator. The angle of FE to BCG is then maintained by the linkage $CEFG$ and this is transferred to the angle of the bucket. In the words of JCB's own publicity material 'The robust loader arms are self-levelling with parallel linkage...'

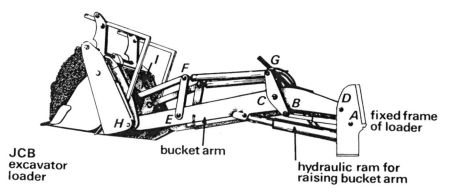

JCB excavator loader

bucket arm

hydraulic ram for raising bucket arm

Pantograph

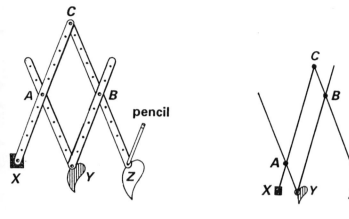

pencil

Another use of the parallelogram linkage is in the drawing instrument known as a *pantograph* which is used for copying drawings and maps to a different scale, or in a different role for guiding a cutting tool in a manufacturing process.

In the left hand diagram above $AYBC$ is a rhombus and $AX=BZ$ and both are equal to the side of the rhombus. The result is that no matter how the linkage is moved X, Y and Z will always be in a straight line with $XY=YZ$. With the pantograph used as shown, X is a fixed point, Y traces around an object and a pencil inserted at Z will make a copy of the object which is an enlargement from X with a linear scale factor of 2. The scale factor of 2 arises because Z is always twice as far from X as Y is. The right hand drawing diagramatically shows the pantograph set up to produce an enlargement from X with a linear scale factor of 4. To achieve this $AC=3AX$, $AC=BY=BZ$ and $AX=AY=CB$. This ensures that X, Y, Z stay in a straight line and $YZ=3XY$, so making $ZX=4YX$.

In general when X is the fixed point and the object is traced out by Y then

$$\text{linear scale factor of the enlargement} = \frac{ZX}{YX}$$

Perhaps the best way to see how the pantograph works is to see its bars as part of a trellis of rhombuses, the kind you can buy in garden centres for training plants on. With this image in mind it is possible to identify other ways of making linkages to produce an enlargement. The figure shows 6 ways of making a linkage to ensure that X, Y and Z are *collinear* (i.e. in a line) and such that $YZ=2XY$.

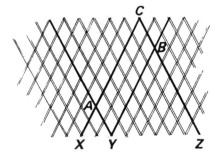

In each of these, if X is the fixed point and an object is traced out with Y, then the image traced by Z will be an enlargement from X with a linear scale factor of 3. If, however, Z traces out the object and the pencil is put at Y, the image will be smaller and an enlargement from X with linear scale factor $\frac{1}{3}$. Note the term enlargement is still used even though the image is smaller.

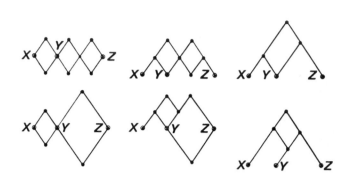

But the story does not end there, for we can take either Y or Z as the fixed point and in each case be left with two choices for where to put the pencil.

A negative scale factor occurs when the image undergoes a 180° rotation about the fixed point as well as an enlargement, and is produced by the above linkages when Y is fixed.

How would you use one of the linkages pictured to produce an enlargement with a linear scale factor of (a) -2, (b) $-\frac{1}{2}$, (c) $\frac{3}{2}$, (d) $\frac{2}{3}$?

To investigate what happens when one enlargement is followed by another it is very enlightening to make up two linkages for enlargements and let the follower of one be the driver for the other.

The figure below illustrates further how the linkages can be used to demonstrate the products of directed numbers. The enlargement from O_2 with a linear scale factor of -2 combined with the enlargement from O_3 with a linear scale factor of -3, is shown to be equivalent to an enlargement from O_1 with a linear scale factor of $+6$, demonstrating

$$-2 \times -3 = -6$$

Note also that the fixed points O_1 O_2 and O_3 are collinear.

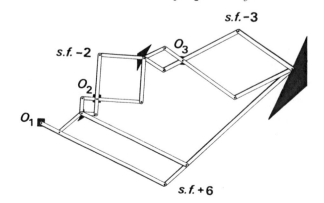

Exercise 4

1 Make a 2-dimensional model of a sewing box or tool box to see how the drawers are linked together. Try to examine an engineer's tool box and see how the handle has been attached in such a way that when it is lifted the drawers are automatically closed. Add such a mechanism to your model.

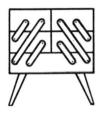 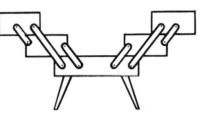

2 Make pop-up greetings cards for a special occasion by sticking card parallelograms onto the card backing as shown. Then stick cut-outs from magazines or old greetings cards onto the fronts of the parallelograms to form a three-dimensional scene.

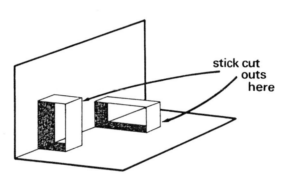

stick cut outs here

3 Design a page of a mobile toy book in which 2 rowers row in unison as a tag projecting from the side of the page (from behind) is manipulated to and fro.

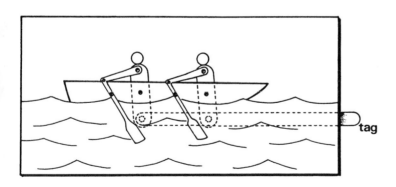

tag

4   Make a model of the street elevator using card and
    geostrips and see how the bucket angle remains
    unchanged no matter how the two arms are orientated.

5   Make a model of the JCB excavator loader lifting
    mechanism, and by manipulating it see how the 4-bar
    linkages maintain the angle of the bucket relative to the
    horizontal, once the length of the hydraulic ram *GF*,
    which controls the angle of the bucket, is set.

6   Fix 3 card strips or
    geostrips *DA*, *AB* and
    BC together using paper
    fasteners at *A* and *B*.
    Then fasten the strips *AD*
    and *BC* to a piece of card
    as shown so that *AB*=*DC*
    and *AD*=*BC* to form a
    parallelogram which can
    be moved to and fro like
    a children's swing.
    Investigate the paths of
    points such as *P*, *Q*, *R*, *S*
    and *T* by making small
    holes in the strips and
    tracing their paths with a
    pencil.

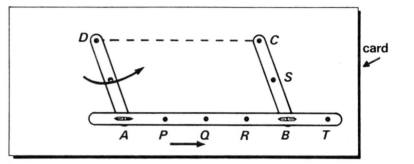

         When *AD* makes an
    angle of 60° with *DC*, in
    what direction will *Q* be
    moving?

7   Make a linkage as shown where *AF*=*BE*=*CD*, *AB*=*FE*
    and *BC*=*ED*=2*AB*.
    (a) Fix *BE* and move *AF*. How does *DC* move?
    (b) Fix *AF* and move *BE*. How does the movement of
        CD compare to the movement of *BE*? What can
        you say about the movement of points on the linkage
        (i) between *BC*, (ii) between *AB*, (iii) between *CD*?
    (c) What movement is possible if you fix *F* and *B*?

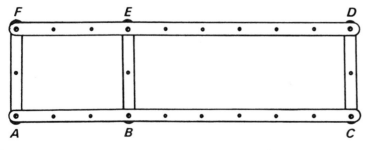

8 A linkage is made as shown in the figure consisting of two interlocking parallelograms, $GC=2CF$ and $DC=3CB$.

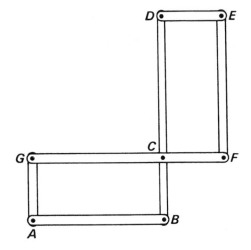

(a) Fix GF and push AB to the right. How does DE move compared to AB?

(b) Fix BD and push AG up. How does EF move compared to AG?

(c) Fix C and let A trace out a straight line. Describe the *paths* followed by G, B, D and F. What other point of the linkage will trace out a straight line? Investigate the locus of E.

(d) Make a model of the linkage to test the validity of your answers.

9 A linkage for enlarging drawings consists of 3 interlinked rhombuses as shown on the right where the long bars such as PQ are 3 times the length of the short bars such as XP.

(a) If X is fixed and an object is traced out by Y, what will be the enlargement factor for the image traced out by (i) Z, (ii) T?

(b) How can the linkage be used to give an enlargement with scale factor (i) $\frac{1}{4}$, (ii) $\frac{3}{4}$, (iii) $\frac{3}{2}$, (iv) $\frac{2}{3}$, (v) -2, (vi) $-\frac{1}{3}$?

10 Design 3 different linkages capable of enlarging with a scale factor of 4.

11 The linkage PAQ on page 66 when fixed at A is such that Q will produce an image of whatever is traced by P equivalent to a half turn rotation about A. Similarly, the linkage QBR when fixed at B is such that R will produce an image of whatever is traced by Q equivalent to a half turn about B.

(a) Test these assertions by making models of the linkages.

(b) Now join the two linkages as shown below so that the output of one is the input of the other and, by trying it out with suitable objects, find the relation between the object traced by *P* and the final image traced by *R*.

These linkages demonstrate very clearly a fundamental theorem in transformation geometry about the combination of two half turns. What do you think it is?

12. A children's jumping frog toy is made from a cardboard linkage and cut-out as shown. The distance between the paper fasteners on each bar of the linkage is about 4 cm. Because of the width of the card strips, the movement of the linkage is limited to $30° < θ < 150°$. How high can the frog be made to jump?

13 An industrial robot moves a tool into the appropriate position by controlling the angles of *AB* and *CB* of a parallelogram linkage.
  (a) If *AB* is held horizontally and *CB* turns about *B*, describe the motion of *DT*.
  (b) If *BC* is fixed and *AB* is turned about *B*, describe the motion of *T*.
  (c) If *AB* and *CB* rotate about *B* at the same speed, what is the locus of *T*?

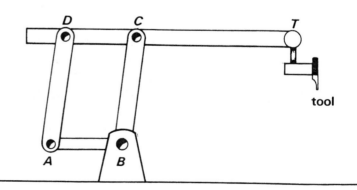

14 The mechanism which moves the tensioning sprockets sideways to make the chain change from one sprocket to another on the free wheel of a derailleur cycle gear consists of a parallelogram linkage. On a typical gear mechanism $AB=DC=1.5$ cm, $AD=BC=4.0$ cm, and the sideways movement required with 5 sprockets

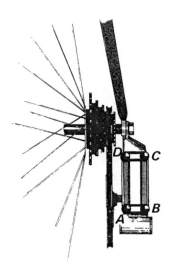

on the free wheel is 2.5 cm. What is the smallest angle through which CB will need to turn to change from the highest gear to the lowest gear?

15 (a) A car's windscreen wiper consists of a blade PQ of length 36 cm attached to an arm AB of length 36 cm which oscillates about A from an angle of 40°, through an angle of 140°, to the horizontal and back as shown in the figure. Assuming that B is the midpoint of PQ, find the area of the windscreen swept out by the blade, to the nearest square centimetre.

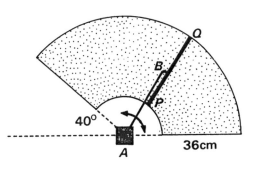

(b) The windscreen wiper on a coach has its blade PQ, of length 40 cm, attached to a parallelogram linkage $ABCD$, which always maintains the blade

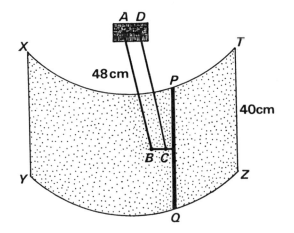

in a vertical position. The lengths of the arms AB and DC are 48 cm, and they oscillate to and fro to reach an angle of 60° to the vertical.
Explain why (i) P and Q both move on arcs of circles of radius 48 cm and (ii) the area swept out is equal to that of a rectangle with dimensions 96 sin 60° cm and 40 cm.

(c) Investigate the area swept out by the windscreen wiper described in (b) if it sweeps through the same angle as before (120°) but the oscillations are not symmetric about the vertical.
(See *Even More Mathematical Activities* Activity 132 commentary, for a discussion of the general case.)

16 In a modern hospital the light over each patient's bed is attached to the wall by two parallelogram linkages as shown. The bracket to which A and D are fixed can turn about a vertical axis, but all other movement of the light is controlled by the movement of the parallelograms.
(a) Why will CE and GF always be at the same angle to the horizontal?
(b) What effect will increasing the angle of AB to the horizontal have on (i) the position and (ii) the angle of the light?
(c) How can the angle of the light be changed?

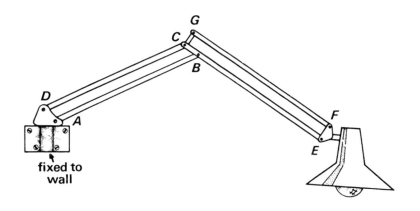

17 Examine an anglepoise lamp and with the aid of a diagram describe the purpose of the design.

*18 A pair of lazy tongs is designed as shown from a line of interlocking rhombic linkages. If X and Y are squeezed together the fingers P and Q of the tongs also come together, but at the same time they will be moving away from the handles surprisingly quickly.

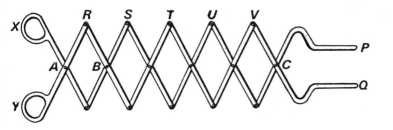

(a) If A is fixed and the handles are squeezed to move B 2 cm to the right, how far to the right will R, S, T, U, V and C move?

(b) The locus of R will be part of a circle whose centre is A. What will be the loci of S, T, U and V?

(c) How is the length of AC related to the distance between the handles?

(d) If X and Y are squeezed together at a constant speed, show that the speed with which C moves away from A increases.

19 Make a parallelogram linkage. Fix AB and cross CD over AB. Now make D turn about A and observe the motion of C. This is known as an antiparallel linkage.

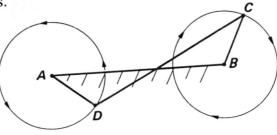

20 Make a parallelogram linkage and move it into the cross-over position as shown. Ideally it should be made with card strips and paper fasteners, and slots cut down the middle of BC and AD. In overlapping the strips at the vertices follow the pattern shown to allow the linkage its full movement. Now fix AB over a piece of paper on a drawing board and carefully trace out the path of the point P where the strips BC and AC intersect. It will be an ellipse because $AP+BP$ is of constant length equal to AD. (See page 31 for an application of this to elliptic gear wheels.)

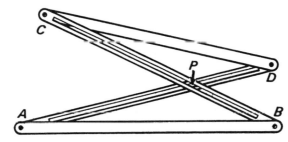

21 Marley folding doors are often suspended by a mechanism which ensures that the doors fold evenly across their width. See if you can design such a mechanism.

5 From rocking horses to steam engines

Applications of the isosceles trapezium linkage

Rocking horses

Children's rocking horses have been designed in principally two ways, to supposedly simulate the motion of a horse. One way is to have curved runners while the other way is to use a trapezium linkage.

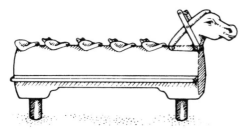

Make up a trapezium linkage $ABCD$ as shown, using card strips and paper fasteners, where AD and BC are of equal length. Hold DC and move AB to and fro. You will notice that as AB moves to the right from the position shown, A moves upwards on a circular arc centred at D, while B moves downwards on a circular arc centred at C, thus giving AB a rocking motion. The 'Tom Cobley' rocking horses seen in children's playgrounds are based on this mechanism, as are many traditional rocking horses. The points D and C correspond to the tops of two posts fixed in the ground and two bars DA and CB are pivoted to these points and to points A and B which are in the body of the horse, to form a trapezium.

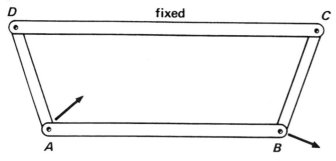

The term *trapezium* linkage is rather a misnomer, for the linkage is only a trapezium when in the symmetric position shown. However it is a convenient name to the 4-bar linkages which have one pair of opposite bars of equal length.

This linkage is also used for see-saws by some manufacturers of playground equipment. In this case the plank of the see-saw, which is long compared to the bars of the linkage, is fixed to DC, and A and B are fixed to the central pillar. This has the advantage that the plank stops turning when DCB is a straight line, thus preventing the end from banging the ground.

Seen only as a mechanism for a rocking horse, the isosceles trapezium linkage would not be significant, but as long ago as 1818 the German engineer Ackermann saw it as the solution to a steering problem for horse drawn coaches which is still used today in the steering mechanism of nearly all wheeled transport. The problem to be overcome is illustrated below, which takes a birdseye view of the direction of travel of the wheels of a car when it is rounding a right hand bend. With very few exceptions the rear wheels of a car point straight ahead, so if they are to roll smoothly over the ground without any sideways drag, the centre of the turning circle, O, must lie along the line of the rear axle. Similarly, if the front wheels P and Q are not to suffer sideways drag they must be rolling in a direction at right angles to the lines from them to O. Now the lines PO and QO must necessarily be at an angle θ to one another as soon as the car is not travelling in a straight line, and this angle will increase as the radius of the turning circle decreases. It follows that the front wheels

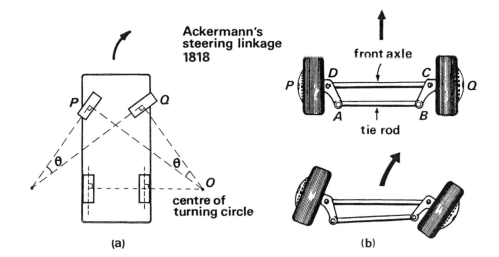

(a) Ackermann's steering linkage 1818 · centre of turning circle

(b) front axle · tie rod

must be at an angle θ to one another, and Ackermann showed how this could be achieved by using a trapezium linkage *ABCD*. Points *D* and *C* are fixed in the car's chassis, while the wheels are pivoted in such a way that their direction is controlled by the bars *AD* and *BC* of the linkage. The relative lengths of the bars of the linkage have to be carefully calculated to give the correct angle θ, and they will depend on the track and wheelbase measurements of the car.

You may need to look quite carefully at the steering mechanism of a modern car to realise that this is the mechanism employed, but it is usually very apparent in a toy go-kart or on a tractor.

Straight line motion

One of the problems which concerned engineers at the end of the eighteenth century and throughout much of the nineteenth century was to find a mechanism which could be used to ensure that the piston rod was pushed and pulled in and out of the cylinder of a steam engine in a straight line (see figure). Without such a mechanism, the connecting rod *PQ* attaching the piston rod to the flywheel pulled the piston rod from side to side and rapidly wore away the bearing at *S*.

James Watt came up with one of the first practical solutions in 1784, based on an isosceles trapezium linkage. He used two long bars *AD* and *BC* and a much shorter bar for *AB*. If *D* and *C* are fixed points (this is equivalent to putting a fourth bar *DC* between them) then for a significant displacement of *AB* from the position shown, the middle point *P* appears to move on a straight line. *Appears* is the operative word, for by making a model of this linkage and tracing out the path of *P* for all the positions which the linkage can take, you will see its limitations! However in practice this linkage was widely used and James Watt considered it his finest achievement.

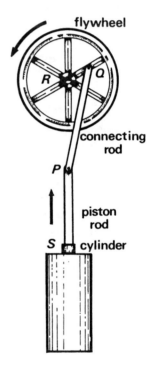

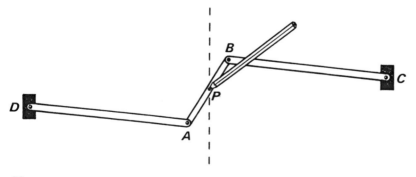

One very clear example of it can be seen at the National Railway Museum in York on a large steam engine, the Weatherhill winding engine (1833), which was used for hauling heavy trucks up a steep incline.

One of the most widely used sources of power for over a hundred years was the Cornish Beam Engine and it was an impressive sight with its large heavy cast iron beam oscillating slowly up and down.

As the beam oscillated (see below) its end point E moved on an arc of a circle so it did not remain in line with the piston rod. To ensure that the end of the piston rod P moved in a straight line, Watt designed a mechanism which incorporated the properties of a parallelogram linkage with his straight line linkage. In the diagram $DA=AE=BP=BC$ and $AB=EP$. C is a fixed point, so that $DABC$ forms a Watt straight line linkage with Q moving in a straight line vertically. Now $ABPE$ is a parallelogram linkage, so AB is always parallel to EP. Also as $DA=AE$ it makes DEP similar to DAQ, so the motion of P is an enlargement of the motion of Q with centre D and linear scale factor 2. As Q moves vertically in a straight line it follows that P will do also.

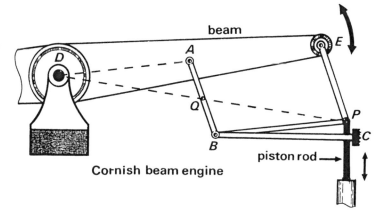

Cornish beam engine

In 1850 a Russian mathematician, Tchebycheff, found another solution to the problem. He used an isosceles trapezium linkage in a crossed over form as shown. In this solution $BC=AD$ and the distances involved are such that

$$AD : CD : AB = 5 : 4 : 2.$$

Again the mid-point P of AB is the one whose locus appears to be a straight line, and a very good approximation it is too for a considerable displacement from the symmetric position shown. However its complete locus is more like a semicircle!

A third solution giving an approximation to straight line motion is that due to the Englishman Richard Roberts who in 1860 proposed the mechanism shown in the figure, also based on a trapezium linkage. But this time instead of considering the locus of the mid-point of AB, an isosceles triangle ABP is attached to AB such that

$$CB=BP=PA=AD.$$

Experimentally this seems to give the best approximation to a straight line of those considered, but paradoxically its complete path wanders furthest from it.

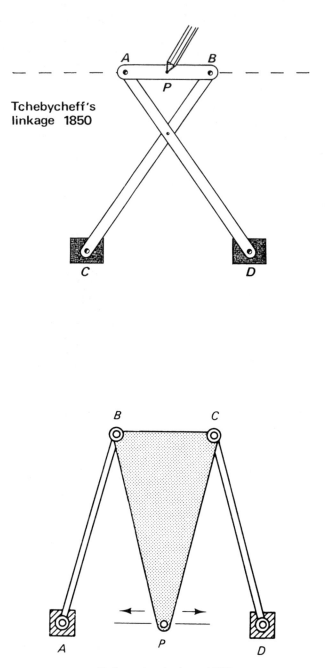

Tchebycheff's linkage 1850

Roberts' solution, 1860

74

Another use for a mechanism to give straight line motion is in the design of a frame saw. With the design in the figure, based on a parallelogram, the saw blade will oscillate up and down, but because C and D are moving on arcs of circles centred at X and Y as the blade moves up and down it will be also moving to left and right, towards and away from the wood being cut.

One way to overcome this problem is to attach the ends of the saw blade to Tchebycheff linkages, and one of my colleagues has built himself a successful fret saw doing just that.

Modern engineers have produced an even more sophisticated solution. In the 1970s a group of Swedish engineers designed a mechanism so that each end of the saw blade moved on a figure-of-eight path so that it cut in one direction but moved clear of the wood when returning to make the next cutting stroke.

In designing suspension systems for heavy vehicles it is necessary to allow vertical displacement of the axles without lateral movement. One way of achieving this is as shown below using a Watt's linkage and coil spring. It has also been incorporated into the rear suspension of modern cars which have been praised for their road-holding characteristics.

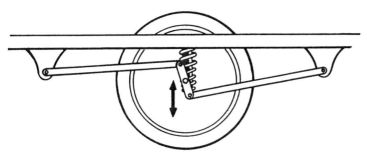

No discussion of straight line motion is complete without a look at Peaucellier's solution. Peaucellier was a French army officer and his solution, which he published in 1864, appeals particularly to the mathematician as it gives, theoretically, an exact straight line. His solution consists of a rhombic linkage $APBQ$ joined at A and B by equal arms to a fixed point O.

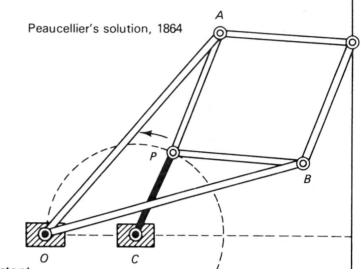

Peaucellier's solution, 1864

Using Pythagoras' theorem it is not too difficult to show that

$$OP \times OQ = OA^2 - AP^2 = \text{constant}$$

and this implies that the relation between P and Q is inversion with respect to a circle centred at O. Further, a property of inversion is that if P traces out a circular path through O, then its image Q will trace out a straight line. It is easy to make P travel on such a circle by fixing it to a rod PC. The theory of this may be beyond readers of this book, unless they are familiar with the complex transformation $Z \to \frac{1}{Z}$, but it is easy to construct Peaucellier's linkage and convince yourself of its unique properties practically.

Although Peaucellier's is theoretically a perfect solution to finding a mechanism for generating straight line motion, in practice it has too many joints and is not as reliable or accurate as the simpler ones discussed based on trapezium linkages.

All the questions in the following exercise involve making models. For many of these Meccano or geostrips are ideal, but very satisfactory models can be made using stiff card and paper fasteners. Large demonstration models can be constructed making use of plastic trellis, sold in garden centres for training plants, and suitably sized nuts and bolts. When making models it is worth remembering that larger models, within reason, will give better results than small ones, for small errors in measurement or play in joints will not be so significant.

Exercise 5

1 Make a model of a Tom Cobley playground horse by first cutting out a card horse and then using card strips AD and BC and paper fasteners to attach the horse to a background sheet of card. Note that D and C are fastened to the background card while A and B are fastened to the horse.

Would the motion of the horse be different if DC was made shorter than AB?

Given that $DC = 1$ m, $AB = 0.8$ m and $DA = CB = 0.2$ m, find the angle of AB to the horizontal when
(i) D, A and B are collinear;
(ii) DA is horizontal;
(iii) AB and DC bisect each other.

Tom Cobley horse

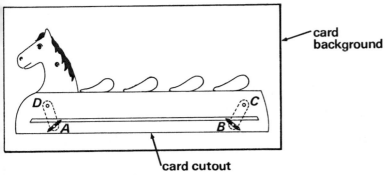

2 Make a model to demonstrate Ackermann's steering linkage as shown. Each wheel and bar to the tie rod is cut from card as a single piece. Points D and C can be fastened to a drawing board using drawing pins, or alternatively they can be fastened to a piece of background card using paper fasteners as in question 1.

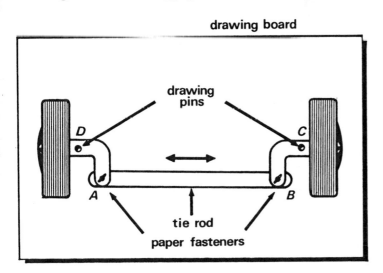

3 Make a Watt's linkage using geostrips or card strips and
fix the end points D and C to a drawing board with
drawing pins. Use a pencil to trace out the complete
locus of the middle point P, of AB. Investigate what
happens to the locus as you vary the distance between
C and D. How does the ratio of the length of AB to the
arms DA and BC affect the locus?

What determines the angle of the straight line portion
of the locus of P to the line joining C to D?

4 Make a model of the
Weatherhill winding
engine using card and
paper fasteners (see the
figure). The paper
fasteners at A, B, C and
D are fixed to the
background card. The
fasteners at P, Q, R and
S move around relative to
the background card so
are better inserted from
the back so that their
pointed ends are visible
and do not scratch the
background. The piston
rod is made by having a
slit in the rod which
allows it to slide past C.
A card washer at C will
prevent the fastener from
pulling through the slit.
A card cylinder can be
added over the top of the
lower end of the piston
rod if desired.

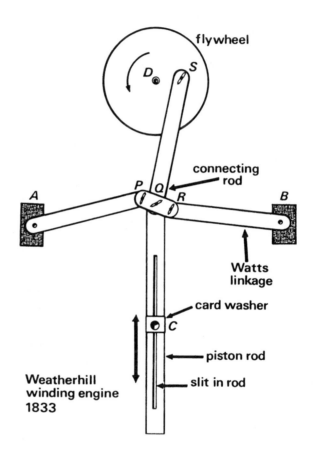

flywheel

connecting rod

Watts linkage

card washer

piston rod

slit in rod

Weatherhill
winding engine
1833

5 Use Meccano or geostrips to simulate the mechanism
designed by Watt for the Cornish Beam Engine. These
magnificent engines can be seen in museums all over
the world. In Britain for example they can be seen at
Poole in Cornwall, Aston and the Iron Bridge Museum
in the Midlands, the Science Museum in London and
last, but not least, the Kew engines which can frequently
be seen working.

6 Make a model of Tchebycheff's linkage and trace the
complete locus of the mid-point of AB. Now vary the

length of AB keeping all the other lengths constant and investigate the family of curves produced.

7 Make a mechanism based on Robert's linkage where the triangle ABP has been replaced by a card strip, and $CD = 2AB$, $BC = AD$. Show that the locus of P is a good approximation to a straight line for a significant part of its path, but diverges widely from it for the remainder.

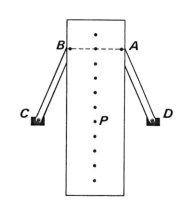

Investigate the paths for other points on the mediator of AB shown by the holes.

8 In the Peaucellier linkage shown earlier the bars of the rhombus were shorter than the bars of the arms from A and B to the fixed point O. The Peaucellier linkage shown in the figure has the relative sizes reversed, but the linkage has essentially the same properties.
   (a) Prove that $OP \times OQ$ is a constant.
   (b) Make a model of a Peaucellier linkage and find the path of Q when P moves on a circle (i) through O, (ii) not through O. To make P move on a circle attach it to another bar whose other end turns about a fixed point.
   (c) What happens to Q if P moves along a straight line?

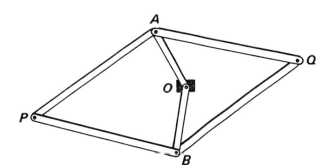

9   Investigate the locus of P and of Q in the linkage illustrated for varying lengths of the bars.

10 The English mathematician Sylvester (1814–97) was fascinated by Peaucellier's linkage for generating straight line motion and determined to find one of his own. The linkage shown in the figure is one of several he devised. This one consists of two similar kites $ACDE$ and $DFBC$, where one has half the linear dimensions of the other. With these dimensions it can be shown that EF is always at right angles to AC, so by fixing F and adding in bar OA so that $OABF$ is a parallelogram, AC always moves parallel to itself, with the result that E moves in a straight line. Make a model and see for yourself.

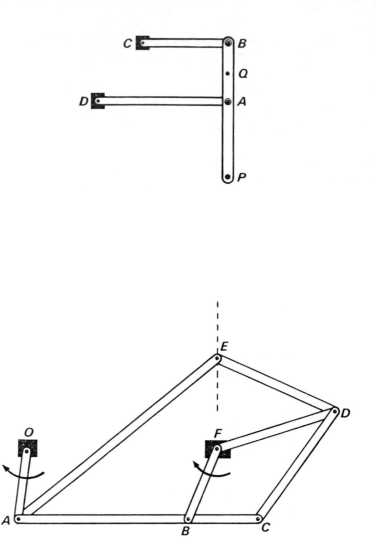

11 The linkage illustrated below shows how a Tchebycheff
    straight line mechanism can be adapted to move a
    platform approximately parallel to itself at the same
    height. The Tchebycheff linkage $ABCD$ is easily
    recognisable and P, the
    mid-point of AB, moves
    approximately on a
    straight line parallel to
    CD. The distance PQ is
    $\frac{1}{2}CD$, R is the mid-point
    of AD and $RQ = \frac{1}{2}AD$.
    Make a model of this
    linkage and test that it
    works.

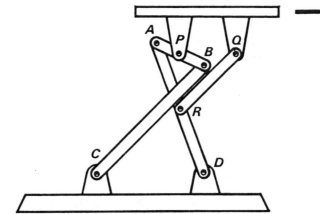

   Sylvester and Kempe designed a linkage which gave
a theoretically exact solution to the translating table
problem, for which Tchebycheff's solution above is an
approximation. Details of this can be found in for
example (a) *Squaring the Circle and other Monographs*
published by the Chelsea Publishing Company in 1969
which contains 'How to draw a straight line; a lecture
on linkages' by A. B. Kempe, or (b) *Machines, an
Illustrated History* by Sigvard Strandh.

12 Honda's 4 wheel steering system is designed so that the
    rear wheels as well as the front wheels change direction
    relative to the chassis, to enable better manoeuvrability
    when turning. Make models to investigate the effect of:
    (a) both sets of wheels turning in the same direction;
    (b) the two sets of wheels turning in opposite directions.

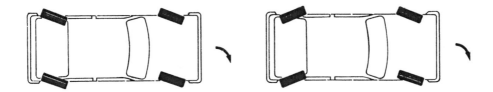

6 Why is a cyclist like a pedal bin?

Applications and analysis of the general 4-bar linkage

In the previous chapters we considered only special cases of a 4-bar linkage where at least two bars were equal in length. In some cases a pair of opposite bars overlapped to form a cross-over linkage, but in most cases the context in which the linkages were used only envisaged a limited range of movement. Now we need to look at the properties of linkages where all the bars are of different lengths and to investigate their range and mode of movement.

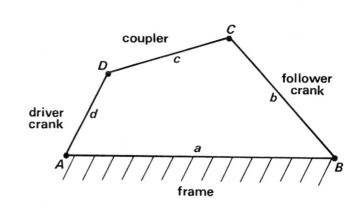

In all applications of 4-bar linkages one bar is fixed and is termed *the frame*; see *AB* in the figure above. The two bars which rotate about the fixed points *A* and *B* are termed *cranks*, while the bar *DC* opposite the frame is called *the coupler*.

The characteristics of a given 4-bar linkage clearly depend on the relative lengths *a*, *b*, *c*, *d* of the bars and which bar is chosen as the frame. For the linkage to exist at all it is clear that no single bar can be longer than the sum of the remaining three, so:

$$a < b+c+d$$
$$b < a+c+d$$
$$c < a+b+d$$
$$d < a+b+c$$

but other relevant inequalities are not so obvious.

Consider the treadle mechanism familiar on old sewing machines and spinning wheels. The points *A* and *B* are fixed pivots in the framework of the machine; the driver crank is the foot treadle; the follower crank is the flywheel; and the coupler is the connecting rod. In this

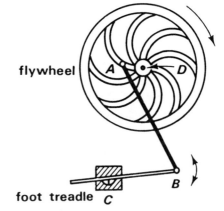

82

application of a 4-bar linkage it is important that the rocking movement of AD leads to the follower crank BC making complete revolutions about B.

Observation suggests that BC is shorter than AD, or is in fact the shortest bar. But is this a necessary condition, and is it a sufficient condition?

The best way to find out is to experiment by making models. When writing this section I found it very helpful to have a box of geostrips always at hand to test various hypotheses and I thoroughly recommend this as a strategy and an aid to thinking creatively about linkages.

Three further applications of this mechanism are shown below. The cyclist is an interesting application, for the cyclist's thigh now performs the role of the driving crank and the lower leg becomes the coupler with the cycle's crank being the follower. The pedal car and the railway trolley used by gangers (made famous in some films) have similar 4-bar linkages and are called *crank and rocker* mechanisms.

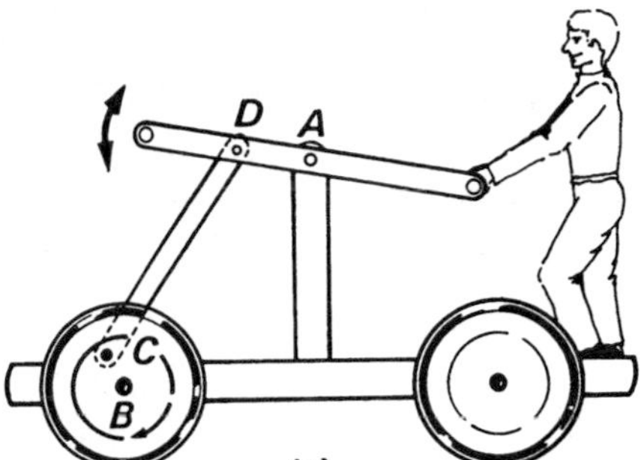

(c)

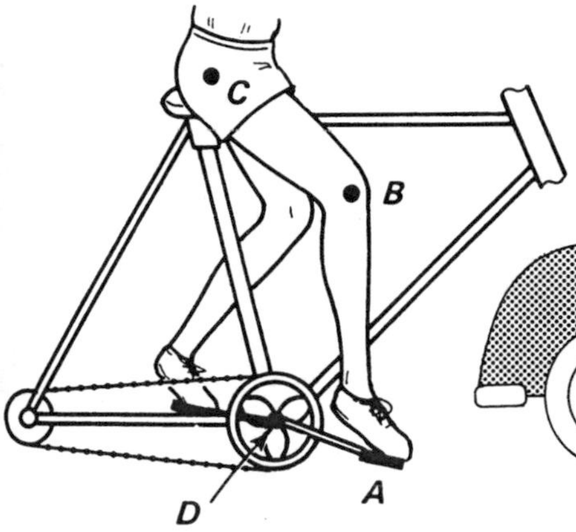

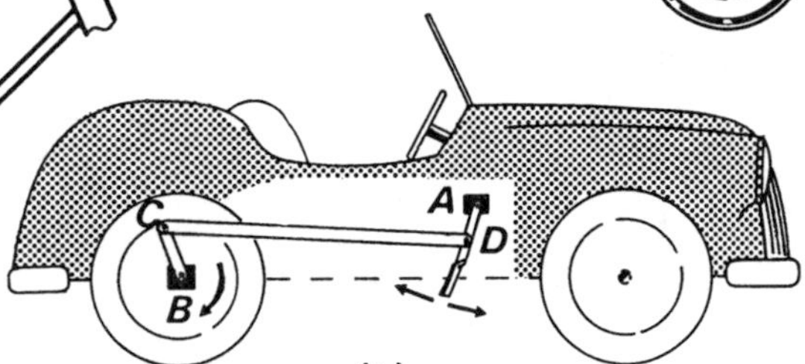

(b)

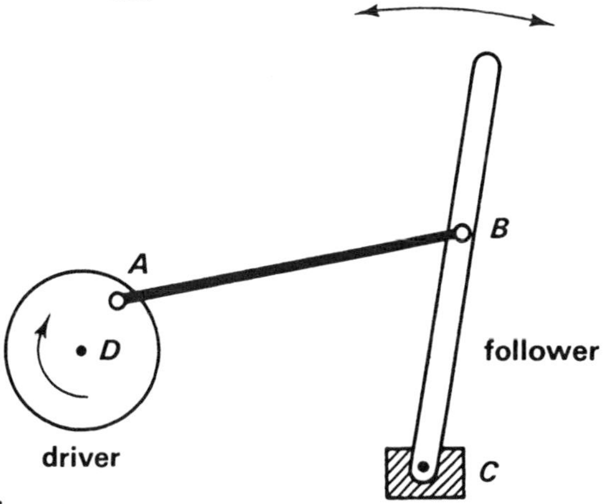

Often the crank and rocker mechanism is used where the driver AD is driven by a constant speed motor and the effect of D travelling in a circle about A is to produce an oscillating motion in the follower BC, hence the term *rocker*.

This mechanism is used widely in industrial machinery where an agitator is required, and could be used to drive the agitator in a domestic washing machine or to produce the to and fro motion of a car's windscreen wipers.

*Grashof's rule

One of the most useful analyses of 4-bar linkages is due to Grashof who in 1883 came to the conclusion that:

> *If the total length of the shortest and longest bars is equal to or shorter than the sum of the lengths of the remaining two bars, then the shortest link can make complete revolutions.*

There are several cases of Grashof's rule to consider.

Case 1

In the example shown the crank AD makes complete revolutions about A and the rocker BC oscillates between the positions BC' and BC''. To find the angle through which BC oscillates note that $AC'=c-d$ and $AC''=c+d$ so all the sides of triangles $AC'B$ and $AC''B$ are known once the lengths of a, b, c and d are known, which enables $\angle ABC'$ and $\angle ABC''$ to be calculated using the cosine rule, or found by scale drawing.

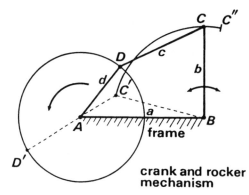

shown with
$a + d < b + c$
but
$b + d < a + c$
and
$c + d < a + b$
are also possible
with d the shortest

crank and rocker
mechanism

Case 2

In this case the conditions on the lengths of the bars are similar to those in the first case, but this time the shortest bar is fixed as the frame, with the result that both cranks AD and BC can make complete revolutions.

It is fascinating to make one of these mechanisms and to observe how the speeds of rotation of the two cranks change relative to one another as the linkage takes up different positions.

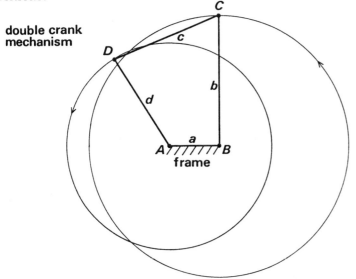

double crank mechanism

frame

Case 3

In the double rocker mechanism the coupler is the shortest bar and can make complete revolutions. But one or other of AD and BC will be the driver and the other the follower, both of which are only capable of a rocking motion.

AD rocks from D', the point distant $b-c$ from B
            to D'', the point distant $b+c$ from B.

Similarly

BC rocks from C', the point distant $d-c$ from A
            to C'', the point distant $d+c$ from A.

In each case the extreme point of the motion occurs when the coupler is in line with one of the cranks.

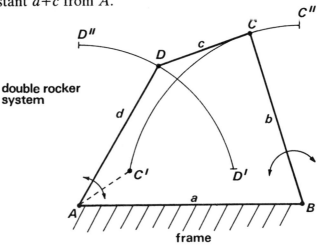

double rocker system

frame

85

*Non-Grashof linkages

When Grashof's rule is not obeyed, that is, the shortest plus longest bars are together longer than the other two bars together, two more cases can be identified.

Case 4

In this case the frame is the longest bar. The rockers oscillate symmetrically about the frame AB and the angles can be easily found by using the cosine rule, or scale drawing.

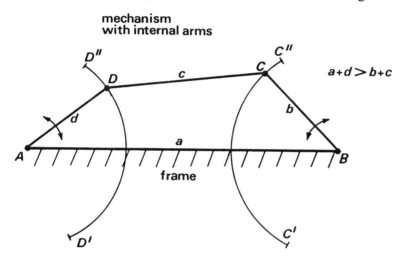

mechanism with internal arms

$a+d > b+c$

Case 5

This time the coupler is the longest bar and the result is that the cranks now rock externally, again with the frame AB as a line of symmetry.

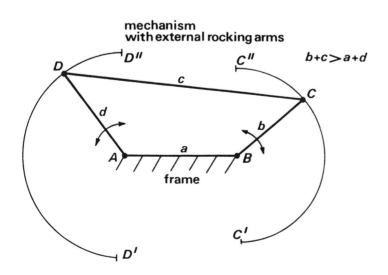

mechanism with external rocking arms

$b+c > a+d$

Exercise 6

1　Make a model of a crank and rocker linkage to represent the treadle mechanism of an old-fashioned sewing machine so that the foot treadle only oscillates through about 30°. How would you modify your model to (i) increase, (ii) decrease the angle of oscillation?

　　If you can inspect an actual treadle mechanism, obtain the measurements of its four bars and the angle through which the foot rest oscillates.

2　Make a 'moving picture', using card and paper fasteners, to represent a cyclist pedalling, or a pedal car, or a ganger's railway trolley complete with ganger.

3　Sometimes a 4-bar linkage is heavily disguised as in a very familiar object, the pedal bin. Here the body of the bin acts as the frame keeping the pivots A and B a fixed distance apart. The bar carrying the pedal is pivoted under the bin at A and is the driver, while the bin's lid is the follower.

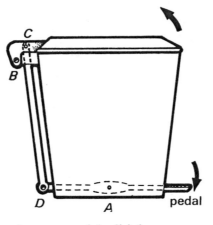

Because the pivot C is nearer the centre of the lid than B the 'linkage' is always operating in a cross-over position where the coupler CD crosses the frame AB. The result is that BC always turns in the opposite direction to AD. Examine a pedal bin and having analysed how it works make a card model to simulate its action.

4　Design a crank and rocker mechanism to drive a car's windscreen wiper through an angle of about 90°.

5　Folding furniture comes in many forms and is particularly useful in modern houses where space is at a premium. Good examples are found in picnic chairs, folding beds, pushchairs and wheelchairs. The following figure depicts the design used on a toy pushchair owned by my daughter. It has a mechanism based on two interacting 4-bar linkages which fold 'flat' as shown when not in use. It is instructive to make a model of this design and to keep a record of other designs you find.

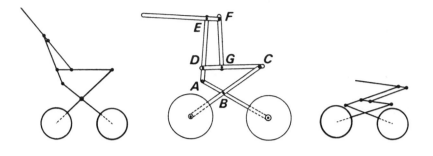

6   Some pruning shears make an ingenious use of the 4-bar
     linkage (see figure (a) below). As the handles are
     squeezed together the cutting blade meets the flat
     cutting surface with a sliding as well as a pincer
     movement, which cuts a stem better than is possible
     with a scissors mechanism. A similar use of the linkage
     for obtaining a close fit is used for the hinge of some
     car bonnets and boot lids, while modern window
     designers are turning to linkages as a way of opening
     windows which will give a good fit when shut but make
     both sides of the glass accessible for cleaning when open
     (see figures (b) and (c)).
        Try to find examples of these uses and find out what
     length bars are used to bring about the required effect.

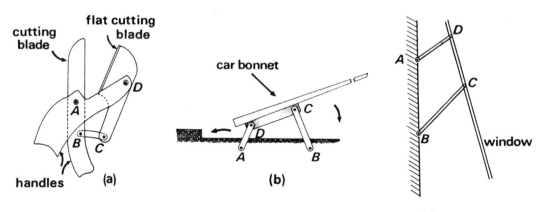

7   When a beam engine was used to drive a winding drum to haul a cage up a mine shaft, the reciprocating motion of the beam was converted into the rotation of a large flywheel by a Grashof rocker-crank mechanism as shown in the figure.

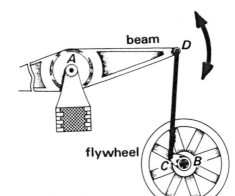

It can be compared to a treadle mechanism of a sewing machine but on a much larger scale. Make a model of a beam engine to incorporate Watt's linkage at one end of the beam and the flywheel at the other.

A good working example of such an engine is in the possession of Kew Bridge Engines Trust in London and is in steam every weekend.

8   One clever use of a 4-bar linkage is as a toggle clamp (see the figure on the right). As the handle is pushed to the left the coupler *CD* lines itself up with *BC* and locks the follower *AD* in position.

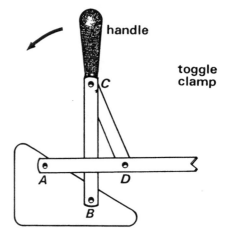

Make a model of this linkage and try to see if it is possible to move *AD* relative to *AB* when *BC* and *DC* are in a straight line.

9   Many doors have mechanisms for automatically closing them after someone has walked through. One such mechanism is based on a 4-bar linkage as shown below. The door frame forms the frame while the door itself is one of the cranks. At *C* the coupler *CD* is attached to a spring which forces the door to close, and a dampening mechanism which prevents it closing too quickly. Inspect one of these mechanisms in use, and by measuring the lengths of the bars of the 4-bar linkage involved find

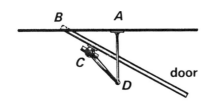

(a) the angle through which the door can open,

(b) the angle through which the spring at C is turned (this will be the variation in the angle between the door and CD).

10 A mole wrench is designed around a 4-bar linkage ABCD and has a screw mechanism S which allows the length of AD to be changed, so altering the ratios of the lengths of the bars of the linkage for different size nuts. It has the property that as BCD approaches a straight line, a large change in the movement of the handles of the wrench produces only a small movement of the jaws, so making it possible to grip a nut very tightly. Make a card model of such a wrench to examine its properties.

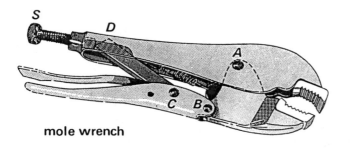

mole wrench

11 The hook of a crane can be moved into a range of positions by the operator. One of the moves available to the operator of a simple jib crane is to increase or decrease the angle of the jib relative to the horizontal, known as luffing (see figure (a)). As jib AB turns about A the hook C will travel on the arc of a circle centre D and radius DC where ABCD is a parallelogram. The effect is to move the hook up or down as well as to move it nearer or further away from the operator. In many situations the crane operator would prefer to achieve a horizontal movement only and this has been made possible by adding a jib lever to the end of a conventional jib (see figure (b)) and a bar BC to complete a 4-bar linkage. As the jib is raised the jib lever turns about D so that the height of E stays almost the same.

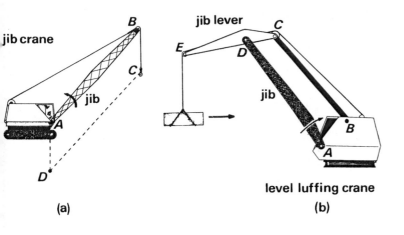

jib crane

B

C

jib

A

D

(a)

jib lever

E

C

D

jib

B

A

level luffing crane

(b)

(i) Make a model of a jib AB out of card, and suspend
a weight C from its end B against a sheet of paper.
Rotate the jib about A and trace the path followed
by C. Vary the length of the suspension to C and
repeat the experiment to verify that C always moves
on a circle of radius AB, with centre below A.

(ii) Experiment with 4-bar mechanisms to simulate the
level luffing crane.

12 Another approximation to straight line motion is
produced by Hoecken's linkage, where the coupler DC
of a crank and rocker mechanism has been extended to
P so that $CP=DC$. The sides of the 4-bar linkage are
in the ratio 2:4:5:5 as shown below and so satisfy
Grashof's rule. Make a model of the linkage and
investigate the paths followed by C and P as the driver
crank AD makes complete revolutions about A.

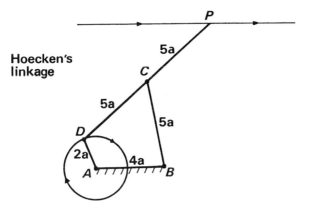

Hoecken's
linkage

P

5a

C

5a

5a

D

2a

A   4a   B

13　Make a 4-bar rocker-crank linkage as shown where the coupler CD consists of a card rhombus, and investigate the paths traced out by different points of the rhombus such as P, Q, R, S and T.

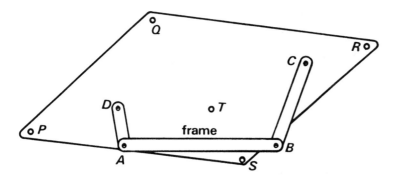

14　Investigate how the angle φ of the follower of a 4-bar linkage changes with the angle θ of the driver. Plot a graph to show this relation for each model you make.

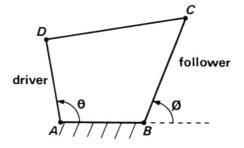

*15　A double rocker mechanism has its four bars in the ratio 4:7:6:2 as shown.

(a) Find the angle of AD to AB at the extreme positions of its motion by making use of scale drawing or the cosine rule. Hence give the angle through which AD can oscillate.

(b) Through what angle can BC oscillate?

(c) What determines which rocker can oscillate through the larger angle?

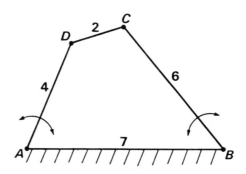

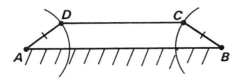

*16 A non-Grashof linkage is to be designed where $AD=BC$ to give internal rocking angles of about 90°. If AB is to be 20 cm give possible lengths for AD, DC and BC. Make a model to test your design.

*17 Design a non-Grashof linkage mechanism with external rocking arms to give rocking angles of 120° given that the frame is 10 cm long.

18 By experimenting with models of 4-bar linkages try to decide if it is possible to manipulate any such linkage into a cyclic quadrilateral.

*19 As a 4-bar linkage is manipulated the area it encloses changes. When does the linkage enclose the largest possible area with a given set of bars?

20 Are there positions for a 4-bar linkage which enable (i) 1 (ii) 2 (iii) 3 (iv) 4 of its interior angles to increase in size as it is manipulated?

21 When a 4-bar linkage is not crossed then the sum of the interior angles is always 360°. Is there a corresponding result for crossed linkages?

22 One mechanism for feeding a ciné film in an intermittent movement from the input of a constant speed motor is to make use of a 4-bar linkage as shown.

   The driver crank AD turns at a constant speed and the end P of the extended coupler DC follows a path which is harnessed to pull the film through one frame by a claw which engages in a perforation in the film for the 'straight' part of its path. Experiment with models of this linkage until you find the correct dimensions to give the required effect.

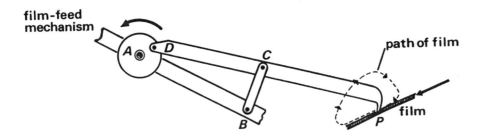

23 Lothar Meggendorfer became famous for his 'Movable Toy' books. The pictures below show an example of his work. When the tab at the bottom of the page is pulled down, not only do a leg and both arms move on this dancing fiddler, but his mouth opens and his eyebrows are raised. All the effects are achieved by imaginative use of 4-bar linkages and variable-based triangles. Try making your own moving picture.

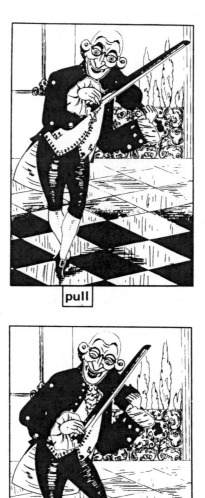

pull

pull

7 Hoist away!

Winding mechanisms

One of the earliest mechanisms recorded is that of a simple winding drum and crank handle, as pictured, for drawing water from a well, and it was in use over 2000 years ago. Clearly the bigger the diameter of the winding drum the more rope will be pulled in for each turn of the crank handle. The significant measurements involved are the radii of the winding drum (r) and of the crank (R).

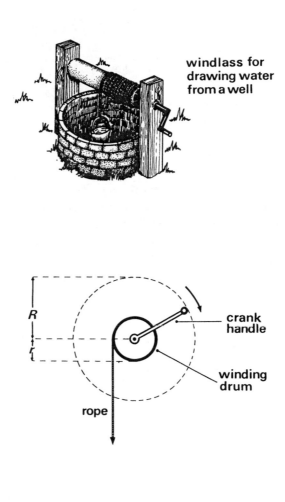

windlass for drawing water from a well

crank handle

winding drum

rope

When the crank handle makes one revolution, the winding drum also makes one revolution. The distance moved by the crank handle in one revolution is $2\pi R$, while the distance moved by a point on the circumference of the winding drum in one revolution is $2\pi r$. The rope will thus be drawn in by a length $2\pi r$ for a distance of $2\pi R$ travelled by the crank handle. The ratio of these two lengths gives the transmission factor of the mechanism.

$$\text{transmission factor} = \frac{\text{distance moved by rope}}{\text{distance moved by handle}} = \frac{2\pi r}{2\pi R} = \frac{r}{R}$$

If no friction were involved then the force required to push the handle compared to the tension in the rope would be proportional to the transmission factor. For example if $r = 4$ cm and $R = 32$ cm then the transmission factor would be $\frac{1}{8}$ so, ignoring friction, the force needed to turn the handle to lift a bucket of water weighing 40 kg weight would be 5 kg weight. But what is gained in having to apply a small force is made up for in the number of turns the crank has to make to haul the bucket to the surface.

When large weights need to be lifted then a simple windlass

will not do, and various methods have been invented to cope with the situation. Often, nowadays, the crank handle will be on a different shaft to the winding drum and linked to it by a gear train to produce a very low transmission factor. The winch shown on the right is typical of those you may see at a fishing port as part of a crane used for lifting boats out of the water, or to pull them up a steep beach to raise them above the tide level, or as a sack hoist for a mill. Similar winches are also to be seen on breakdown lorries. On the winch shown, the gears have 15 teeth and 90 teeth respectively so the winding drum only turns once for every 6 revolutions of the crank wheel. To obtain a very low transmission factor further gear wheels can be introduced – even a worm gear is sometimes used.

When a gear train is used to connect the crank to the winding drum the overall transmission factor will be given by

$$\text{transmission factor} = \frac{r}{R} \times \text{gear ratio}$$

Thus if the crank handle in the diagram has a radius of 40 cm, and the winding drum a radius of 8 cm, the overall transmission factor for the winch will be

$$\frac{5}{40} \times \frac{15}{90} = \frac{1}{48}$$

I have very clear memories of cranking a primitive winch on a crane and lifting blocks of granite weighing up to 3 tonnes, when I was only ten years old.

Before gear wheels were in general use however the pulley wheel had been invented and widely exploited. In fact Archimedes (287–212 BC) is thought to have invented the compound pulley, and this mechanism is used widely to this day on sailing ships, cargo boats, and cranes and hoists of all kinds.

Consider the simple pulley system shown in figure (a). If the rope at P is pulled a distance of d metres along its length then Q will be raised through d metres, so the transmission factor will be given by

96

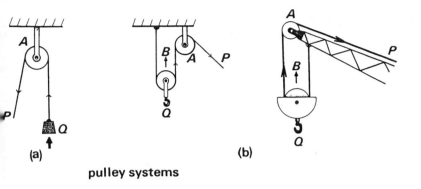

pulley systems

$$\frac{\text{distance moved by } Q}{\text{distance moved by } P} = \frac{d}{d} = 1$$

Now consider the pulley systems used in figure (b). For the hook Q to be raised through d metres the rope on both sides of the pulley B will be shortened by d metres which means that P will need to be pulled through a distance of $2d$ metres. Hence the transmission factor will be

$$\frac{\text{distance moved by } Q}{\text{distance moved by } P} = \frac{d}{2d} = \frac{1}{2}$$

By increasing the number of pulleys to N the transmission factor can be reduced to $\frac{1}{N}$. The figure on the right shows the special case where $N = 4$. To see why the transmission factor is $\frac{1}{4}$ in this case, imagine the pulley block containing pulleys B and D raised through d metres. Then the 4 sections of rope between the two pulley blocks will all be shortened by d metres, which can only be achieved by P being pulled a distance of $4d$ metres.

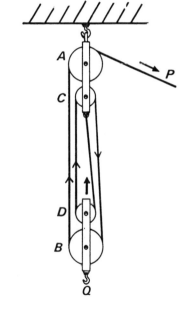

Models of these pulley systems can easily be made from the standard construction kits but satisfactory models can be made by using pulleys made from cardboard circles stuck together.

card circles

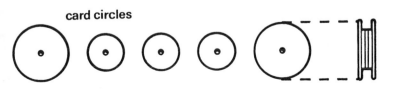

97

Alternatively the humble paper clip can be used to represent a pulley block as shown below which represents a system with a transmission factor of $\frac{1}{3}$.

In practice pulley blocks usually come with the pulleys side-by-side on the same shaft. In the sailing era, when sailing clippers carried cargoes all over the world, a typical large ship might require up to 1000 blocks. These were made of wood, by hand, until the famous French engineer Marc Isambard Brunel invented machines to mechanise the process in 1803. The result was that in a very short time the British navy's annual requirement of 130,000 pulley blocks was being produced by 10 men instead of the 110 previously employed. Modern sailing boats still employ pulley blocks, but now they are made of metal.

Another simple device for obtaining a large or small transmission factor is to have two winding drums turning together on the same shaft, so that as the rope is wound in on one drum it is being unwound from the other. If the radius of A is a and the radius of B is b, then in n revolutions of the drums P will move a distance $2n\pi a$ and Q will move a distance $2n\pi b$. It follows that the transmission factor will be

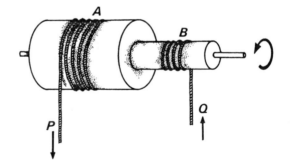

$$\frac{\text{distance moved by } Q}{\text{distance moved by } P} = \frac{2n\pi b}{2n\pi a} = \frac{b}{a}$$

A system like this can easily be modelled using a cotton reel and a pencil or dowel. By linking such systems together very high or very low transmission factors can be achieved.

A clever adaptation of this system is to be found in the Weston differential pulley which is widely used to lift heavy loads, such as lifting an engine from a car for major repairs. In this system the rope is usually replaced by a chain, in the form of a continuous loop. As the pulleys A and B rotate together in a clockwise direction (see below) the chain from A to C is wound up but the chain from B to C is unwound. In one revolution of the A–B block P moves a distance $2\pi a$, while the loop of chain from A around C and back to B has been shortened by $2\pi a - 2\pi b$. The effect of this is to raise Q through $\frac{1}{2}(2\pi a - 2\pi b)$, that is through $\pi(a - b)$. The transmission factor of Q relative to P is thus

$$\frac{\text{distance moved by } Q}{\text{distance moved by } P} = \frac{\pi(a - b)}{2\pi a} = \frac{a - b}{2a}$$

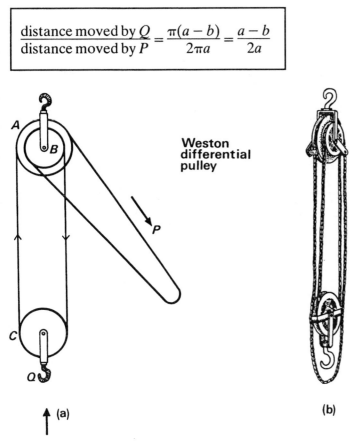

Weston differential pulley

(a)

(b)

To see the effectiveness of this system consider the situation where $a = 8$ cm and $b = 7.5$ cm, then

$$\frac{a - b}{2a} = \frac{8 - 7.5}{16} = \frac{0.5}{16} = \frac{1}{32}$$

So Q only moves 1 cm for every 32 cm moved by P.

When you watch someone operating a Weston differential pulley you will be aware of them pulling what seems to be an endless length of chain at P to achieve a small change in the height of Q, but large loads can be lifted at Q as a result.

Exercise 7

1 A simple windlass has a winding drum of radius 9 cm and the crank handle has a radius of 36 cm. Find how fast the rope is being wound onto the drum when the crank handle is turned at 1 revolution per second. How fast is the winder's hand moving compared to the speed of the rope?

2 The crank of a winch is connected to a shaft carrying sprocket A with 12 teeth. Sprocket A engages sprocket B with 36 teeth which turns sprocket C on the same shaft with 16 teeth. Sprocket C engages sprocket D with 64 teeth which is on the same shaft as the winding drum W. The radius of the crank is 40 cm and the radius of the drum is 10 cm. What is the transmission factor of the rope Q relative to the crank handle?

3 Design a pulley system using 3 wheels with a transmission factor of $\frac{1}{3}$.

4 In the pulley system shown the pulleys A and C turn about fixed shafts but B and D can move. Find the transmission factor of Q relative to P. If a load is to be lifted by Q through a height of 12 metres, how far will the rope at P need to be pulled?

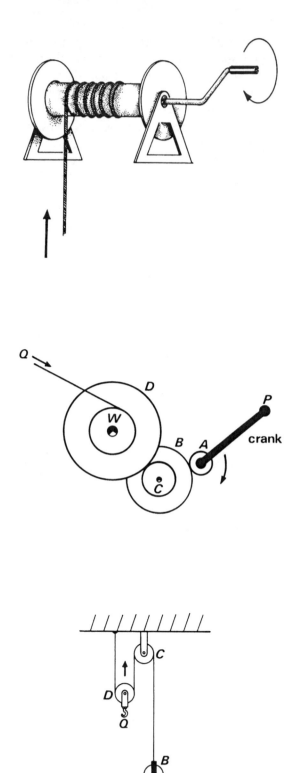

5 (a) Design a pulley system using 6 pulley wheels to have a transmission factor of $\frac{1}{6}$.

(b) How could a pulley system using only 5 pulley wheels be designed with the same transmission factor? (*Hint.* 2×3=6)

6 Find the transmission factor of Q relative to P in the pulley system illustrated. What would the factor be if another pulley was added in the same way?

Can you establish a general result for N pulleys linked together in the same way?

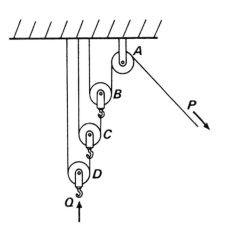

7 Design a pulley system with a transmission factor of $\frac{1}{12}$. There are several different solutions. Which uses the smallest number of pulley wheels?

8 Five winding drums A, B, C, D and E with radii 4 cm, 12 cm, 4 cm, 20 cm and 4 cm respectively are linked by ropes as shown. Given that the crank handle has a radius of 20 cm find the transmission factor of Q relative to P.

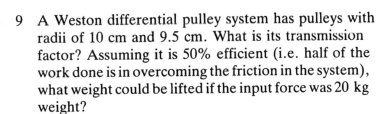

9 A Weston differential pulley system has pulleys with radii of 10 cm and 9.5 cm. What is its transmission factor? Assuming it is 50% efficient (i.e. half of the work done is in overcoming the friction in the system), what weight could be lifted if the input force was 20 kg weight?

10 Given that a Weston differential pulley system has a transmission factor of 1:50 what is the radius of the larger pulley if the smaller pulley has a radius of 12 cm?

11 Make a note of the use of pulley blocks and winches
you see on
(a) tower cranes on building sites;
(b) gantry cranes in engineering works;
(c) dockside cranes;
(d) derricks on cargo boats;
(e) sailing boats;
(f) canal banks, often near lock gates;
(g) pitheads of mines;
(h) sack hoists in mills and warehouses;
(i) garages and breakdown lorries;
(j) trailers for boats;
(k) the post for a tennis net;
(l) a fishing rod.
Analyse the transmission factors involved in each case.
Make models to illustrate the mechanisms.

*12 There are many situations where the effective diameter
of a winding drum changes significantly as the material
being wound on builds up on the drum. The reels
holding the film for a ciné-projector or the tape for a
video recorder or cassette tape recorder are typical
examples.

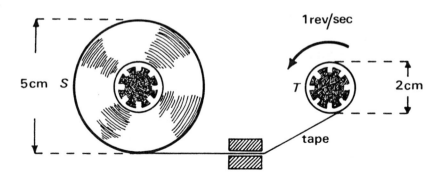

Observation of a typical cassette tape player suggests
that the take-up reel T rotates at approximately one
revolution per second. When empty the diameter of a
typical C60 cassette reel is 2 cm but when full, after it
has been playing for half an hour, the reel plus tape has
a diameter of 5 cm.
(a) How many revolutions does the reel T make in half
an hour?
This gives the number of thicknesses of tape on a
full reel so it is now possible to deduce (i) the
thickness of the magnetic tape, and (ii) the length
of the tape in a C60 cassette.

(b) What is the range of transmission factors of the driver T to the follower S?

(c) Find the radii of the two reels plus tape t seconds from the start and hence derive an expression for the transmission factor as a function of time.

(d) When is the tape travelling at a speed of 11 cm/s? (*Hint.* The length of tape on a reel is proportional to its cross-sectional area.)

*13 When a mine shaft is deep the weight of the rope holding the cage is often heavier than the loaded cage, so that the load on the winding engine varies considerably as the cage is hauled up. One way of equalising the load is to use a winding drum in the shape of a cone, so that its effective radius changes as the cage is raised or lowered. The surface of the cone is grooved and the rope starts winding on it from the small end, when the load is greatest, gradually climbing up the surface of the cone to the larger cross-section as most of the rope is wound in. Cages are usually worked in pairs as a counterbalance, so that one cage goes down as the other comes up.

(a) Given that the small and large diameters of the conical drum are 2 m and 4 m respectively, and that the winding drum makes 100 revolutions to empty or fill, find the approximate length of rope on each half of the drum.

(b) Explain why the distance through which one cage is raised is not normally equal to the distance through which the counterbalancing cage is lowered.

(c) On a graph plot the distances moved by the cages A and B against the number of revolutions of the drum, starting from the point where A is at the bottom and B at the top of the shaft.

conical winding drums

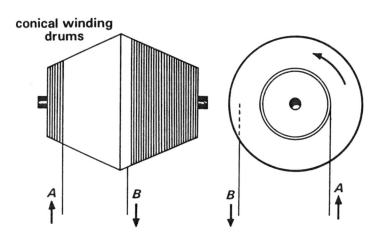

14 It is required to produce a magic box for a conjuror which gives the impression that the string Q can be pulled out of the box twice as fast as it enters at P. How many different mechanisms can you invent to do this?

Now try to produce a box which 'manufactures' 3 times as much string as it consumes!

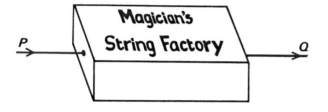

15 Before digital computers became so sophisticated much thought was given to the design of analogue computers, where a quantity could be represented by some physical measurement such as length, voltage, or temperature. One such device was based on wires and pulleys, and a basic ingredient of the computer was a mechanism for adding two linear movements p and q. Design a mechanism to fit in a box so that if two parallel wires are pulled out of one side of the box through distances of p cm and q cm respectively, then a third wire will be pulled into the opposite side of the box through a distance of $(p + q)$ cm.

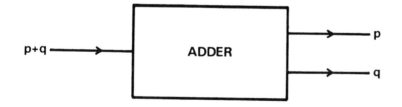

16 The mechanism in the figure has a winding drum A which turns about a fixed axis, and two pulleys B and C whose shafts are attached to a movable frame so that they are constrained to move together.

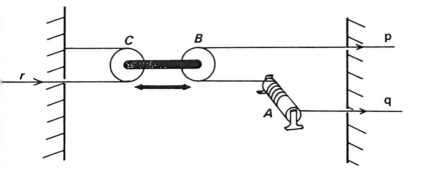

How far does r move when p is pulled 12 cm to the right and q is pulled 7 cm to the right?

What arithmetic operation does this mechanism represent?

17 The figure below shows a railway crane which is typical of the design of cranes which are required to lift heavy loads. In particular, the cranes developed for the oil industry in the North Sea, such as the Heerema floating crane with the prodigious lifting capacity of 5000 tonnes, all depend on the same basic design.

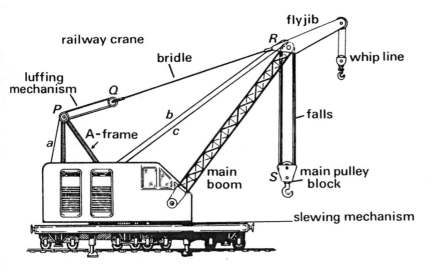

The crane on page 105 has 3 basic winding mechanisms:

(i) The main boom is raised or lowered (known as luffing) by a pulley system which connects the top of the fixed A-frame to the top of the boom, R, via two metal rods or cables, known as the bridle. The pulley blocks for the luffing system may contain many pulleys, so that the cable a will need to be wound in many times the distance through which it is required to shorten PQ. If the tension in the bridle is 120 tonnes weight, and there are 6 pulleys on each of the blocks at P and Q, how many lengths of cable will there be between P and Q?

What length of cable a will need to be wound in to shorten PQ by 1 metre? What will be the tension in cable a?

(ii) The main lifting hook is attached to the pulley block S with 5 pulleys which work in conjunction with 5 pulleys at the end of the boom R. The cable c from the main winding drum passes over the pulleys at R and around the pulleys at S, giving 10 lengths between R and S (known as falls) before being fixed to the end of the boom.

If the crane is lifting a load of 140 tonnes weight, what is the approximate tension in the cable c?

(iii) the hook on the whip line at the end of the fly jib is used for quickly lifting light loads. If the whip line has two falls and cable b is wound in at 4 m/s at what speed will the load be lifted?

8 Rolling along

Rollers and wheels

From very early times people built monuments from large stones, such as the pyramids of Egypt, or Stonehenge, or the monoliths of Easter Island in the Pacific. It is assumed that they used logs as rollers to move them into place.

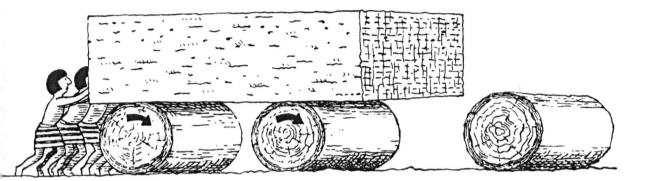

There are two ways in which rollers are used. First consider the situation where the rollers turn around fixed axes (see figure (a)). You will meet this application at airports, for moving baggage, or on a large scale in a steel mill, for moving heavy ingots. If the rollers are of diameter d, then after one revolution every point on the circumference of the rollers will have moved a distance πd and any object being moved by them will move forward the same distance. However, if the rollers themselves are free to roll across the ground (see figure (b)) then the object being moved will have been translated through a distance of $2\pi d$, as the distance moved by the rollers must be added to the distance the object has moved relative to the rollers.

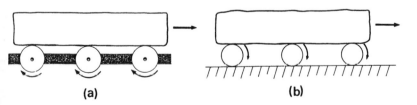

(a)   (b)

The most convincing way to see the last result is to do an experiment using pencils or glue-sticks, or any other convenient cylindrical objects as rollers, and roll a book across the table, measuring the distance moved by the rollers and the book.

The important property of a roller is that it always has the same width no matter in which direction its cross-section is measured. Surprisingly, the circle is not the only shape with this property. An infinity of such curves exist, known as *curves of constant breadth*.

The simplest non-circular members of this family of curves are those based on equilateral triangles and often referred to as *Reuleaux triangles* after the German engineer Franz Reuleaux (1829–1905) who first recorded their properties (see below). If shapes are cut out of card as shown and placed between two parallel rulers placed 5 cm apart, then no matter how the shapes are rotated they will always be touching the two rulers.

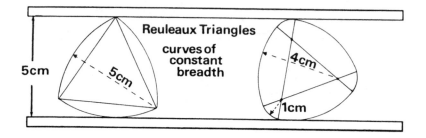

Reuleaux Triangles
curves of constant breadth

Similar shapes can be made based on regular polygons with an odd number of sides and good examples of these shapes are the British 50p and 20p coins based on regular heptagons. Because of their constant breadth property they can be used in slot machines which are designed to accept only one diameter of coin.

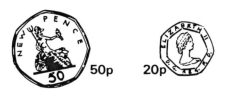

50p   20p

The English engineer Harry James Watts recognised the potential of the Reuleaux triangle in 1914 as the cross-section of a bit for drilling square holes. By cutting away part of the curve to form a cutting edge, and turning the drill inside a square template using a flexible driver shaft (why?) the drill always touched the four sides of the square and cut out a very good approximation to a square hole, only leaving the corners slightly rounded.

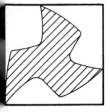

Watt's chuck and drill

The Reuleaux triangle has also been used in the very successful design of the NSU–Wankel rotary engine, where it is used as the cross-section of the rotor. Without the wear and vibration of the reciprocating pistons of a conventional engine the design has great potential. However, as in 1901 when a steam engine was designed on similar lines, there are problems in maintaining a satisfactory seal between the rotor and the cylinder walls.

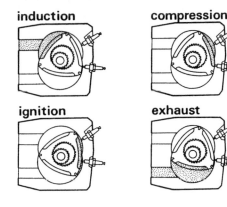

induction   compression

ignition   exhaust

What is perhaps very surprising is to find that curves of constant breadth do not even have to have rotational symmetry. One very effective method for constructing such shapes is to start by drawing any number of intersecting lines. Four have been used in the example on the right labelled l_1, l_2, l_3, l_4. Each arc is then drawn from the point of intersection of the two lines which bound it. For example this shape was drawn by first drawing arc a_1 with an arbitrary radius centred on A.

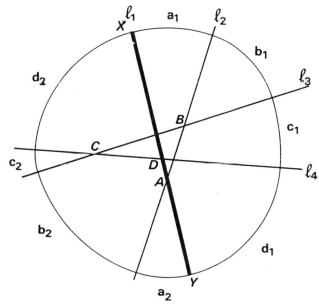

crossed-line constuction of curve of constant breadth

Arc b_1 was then drawn with centre B, arc c_1 with centre C, arc d_1 with centre D and so on, adjusting the radius at each stage to ensure that adjacent arcs meet. To see that this shape has the required property of constant breadth, consider XY, that part of l_1 cut off by the curve. Rotate it clockwise about A to coincide with l_2, then clockwise about B to coincide with l_3 and finally clockwise about C to coincide with l_4. As it rotates, X and Y trace out the curve and establish the constant width property.

What is also interesting to learn is that the perimeter of these shapes is always $\pi \times$ (breadth of shape), thus giving it the same perimeter as a circle with the same diameter.

Rotating shafts and rollers will wear with use in their bearings and will often end up with non-circular cross-sections which are curves of constant breadth.

In steel rolling mills rollers are used to squeeze the white hot ingots of steel into girders and railway lines or whatever section is required. The figure below shows sets of rollers for producing an **I** section and a **T** section. Because the squeezing process reduces the area of cross-section of the metal when it goes through the rollers, the girder coming out will be longer than the ingot entering the rollers. This process is particularly striking when a large cuboid of white hot metal ends up as a long thin sheet of steel, after passing through several sets of rollers each of which reduces its thickness. See what you can find out about the reduction factor at each stage of the rolling.

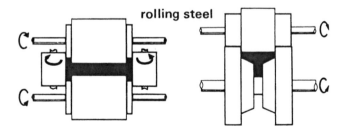

In the woollen industry the spinning process makes much use of rollers, and in particular the carding process uses rollers which are geared so that adjacent rollers are forced to slip relative to one another. Try to visit a woollen mill and see a carder in operation.

Slipping rollers are essential in a surprising situation. The wheels on trains and the rolling stock of railways are fixed rigidly to axles so that the two wheels at the end of a particular axle turn together. If the wheels turn without slipping on their rails then they will both travel forward exactly the same distance. This is fine as long as the track is straight, but if it bends then the distance along the rail on the outside of the bend is longer than the distance along the rail on the inside of the bend. So for an engine and its rolling stock to negotiate a bend, at least one of the wheels on each axle must slip on the railway line.

train wheels

When a cylindrical roller or wheel rolls along a flat surface it is interesting to investigate the velocity of each point of the roller at any instant in time. This can be deduced in several ways, but the most helpful is to realise that, if the roller is not slipping, then its point of contact with the surface, A, is momentarily at rest and it can be thought of as turning about A. Because of this A is called the

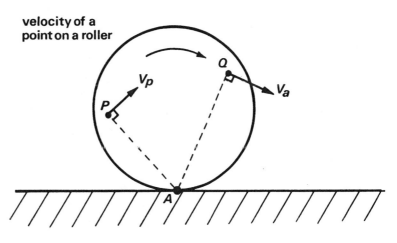

velocity of a point on a roller

instantaneous centre of rotation for the roller. The figure shows the velocities V_P and V_Q of two typical points, P and Q, of the roller. As the roller is turning about A the direction of the velocities of P and Q will be at right angles to AP and AQ respectively. Further, if the angular speed of the roller is ω then $V_P = \omega AP$ and $V_Q = \omega AQ$, so the speed of any point on the roller is proportional to its distance from A.

It is important to appreciate the difference between a wheel or roller turning about a fixed axis and the same wheel or roller with the same angular speed rolling on a flat surface without slipping.

Imagine a roller rotating about a fixed axis so that every point on its surface has a speed of 60 km/h. Then the direction of the velocity of a typical point P will be along the tangent at P for it is at right angles to the line OP from the centre of rotation.

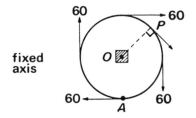

fixed axis

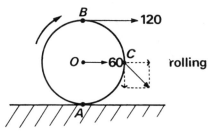

rolling

However, if the roller is turning at the same speed, but rolling on a flat surface, its centre O is now moving with a speed of 60 km/h to the right while A is momentarily at rest. The velocity of any point of the roller can now be found by adding vectorially a velocity of 60 km/h from left to right to the velocity for the same point when the axis O was fixed. Thus B has a velocity of 120 km/h to the right while C has a velocity made up of 60 km/h to the right with 60 km/h down, giving a speed of $60\sqrt{2}$ km/h in a direction of 45° down from the horizontal.

In general it follows that when a car is travelling at a speed of V km/h then the point of each wheel furthest from the road surface is travelling at $2V$ km/h.

Suppose a piece of gravel is picked up by the tyre of a car travelling at 100 km/h, then it will be travelling forward at a speed of 200 km/h when it reaches the top of the wheel, and if it leaves the tyre at that point it could be lethal to anyone in its path!

The path traced out by a point P on the circumference of a rolling wheel is called a *cycloid* and it has many interesting properties, not the least of which is that when inverted it gives the curves of fastest descent for an object sliding without friction from one point to another.

cycloid

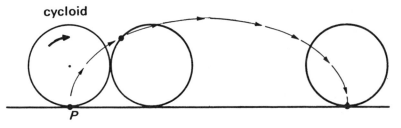

To test this in practice first produce a cycloid by rolling a saucer or tin lid along a straight edge and tracing the path of a point on its circumference. Then cut out a runner in the shape of an inverted cycloid from thick card or hardboard – two identical pieces kept apart by a spacer will provide a path down which you can roll a marble. Next to the cycloidal path make a straight path (see below) and experiment by rolling two marbles down the adjacent tracks so that they start and finish at the same points. You should find that the marble on the cycloidal path always arrives first, even if part of its path is uphill. Comparison with tracks having other profiles using the same technique (or try experimenting with plastic curtain runners) should convince you that the cycloidal track is the fastest.

So far nothing has been said about the distinctive property of a wheel which distinguishes it from a roller, although all our experience suggests that wheels, unlike rollers, need to be circular. To focus on the requirements for a wheel it is important to see that the load carried by a wheel, whether on a car or a lorry or a train, is supported by the axle, and that when the wheel rolls on a flat surface the load should travel in a straight line parallel to the surface. For this to happen the axle must always be at the same distance from the surface, and this will only happen when the wheel is circular and the axle through its centre. The figure below shows the paths followed by the centres of an equilateral triangle and a square as they roll, showing how an axle and its load would bump up and down, so making them unsuitable for wheels.

Exercise 8

1   Make a *Reuleaux triangle* from card with a diameter of
    5 cm.
    (a) Place the triangle
        between two rulers
        fixed 5 cm apart.
        Roll the triangle
        along one ruler and
        see that it always
        touches the second
        ruler.

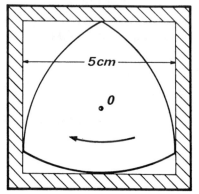

    (b) Make a small hole in
        the centre of the
        triangle and trace its
        locus as the triangle
        is rolled along a ruler.
    (c) Cut a square hole 5 cm by 5 cm from a piece of
        card and fit your triangle into it. Turn the triangle
        and observe that it is always in contact with all four
        sides of the square.

    Further, trace the locus of the centre O of the triangle
    as it turns inside the square.

    Why would a Reuleaux triangle make a poor wheel?

    Why does Watt's drill for square holes require a
    special chuck?

2   Construct curves of constant breadth based on
    (i) a regular pentagon   (ii) a regular heptagon   (i.e. a
    50p piece).
    Estimate the circumference of these shapes by rolling
    suitable cut-outs, or carefully placing cotton around
    their boundaries. Measure the breadth of each shape
    and use your calculator to work out the ratio

    $$\frac{\text{length of boundary of shape}}{\text{breadth of shape}}$$

    to 2 decimal places. Compare with π.

*3 Prove that the perimeter of the two Reuleaux triangles
    shown on page 108 is 5π cm. You can use the result
    that for an arc s of a circle of radius r which subtends
    an angle θ at the centre

    $s = r\theta$ \qquad when θ is in radians

    $s = r\theta \times \dfrac{\pi}{180}$ when θ is in degrees.

114

4 Construct a non-regular curve of constant breadth using the intersecting lines method for 3 lines.
  What happens if you use the method for just 2 lines?

*5 Prove that the perimeter of the curve of constant breadth for the shape drawn on page 109 using 4 intersecting lines is πXY.

6 See where you can find examples of rollers in use such as:
  (a) a clothes mangle/wringer;
  (b) baggage handling at airports;
  (c) lorry loading bays at warehouses;
  (d) steel mills;
  (e) rolling mills for rolling steel plate or girders;
  (f) newspaper printing press;
  (g) for supporting conveyor belts;
  (h) textile printing;
  (i) for moving cans or bottles around a food processing plant.

7 Design a set of rollers suitable for rolling railway sleepers having the cross-section shown.

8 A cone whose base is of radius r and whose slant edge is of length l rolls on a flat horizontal surface.
  Describe what happens to the cone.
  If the cone returns to the same spot after rotating twice about its own axis of symmetry, what can you say about the angle of the cone?

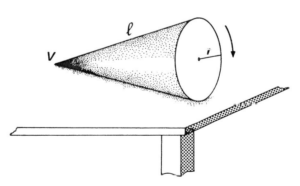

9 The frustum of a cone is such that the diameters of its smallest and largest circular cross-sections are 4 cm and 8 cm. The slant edge of the frustum is 6 cm. Describe, in detail, the area swept out by the roller as it rolls on a flat surface. How many times must the frustum rotate about its own axis before it returns to its starting point?

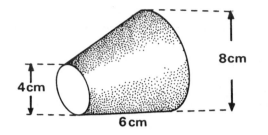

10 A car is being tested in a garage by mounting the driving wheels on rollers A and B (see figure). The driving wheel is 50 cm in diameter and is turning anticlockwise at a speed which would be equivalent to 100 kilometres per hour if the car was on the road. The rollers A and B have diameter 10 cm. Find the angular velocity of the rollers in revolutions per minute.

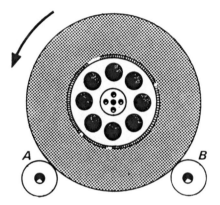

11 A square $ABCD$ is rolled along a straight line. Find the path traced by A as it rolls.

If the square starts rotating about D so that C moves to the right with a speed of 2 m/s what are the initial velocities of A, of B, and of M, the mid-point of BC?

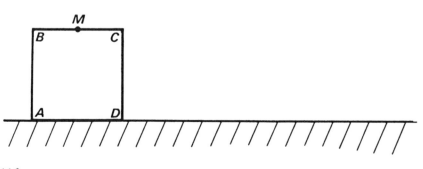

116

12 Investigate the paths of different points of the rectangle and triangle shown as they roll along a straight line.

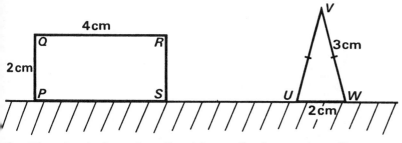

13 The wheel of a train rolls without slipping on the rail as the train speeds along at 200 km/h.
(a) Which point of the wheel is momentarily at rest?
(b) What are the velocities of the points A, B, D?
(c) Do any points have a vertical velocity?
(d) Which points have a speed of 200 km/h?

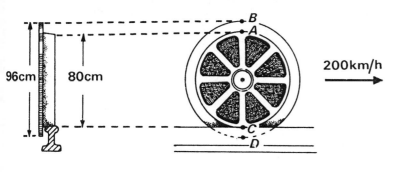

14 Two perpendicular shafts are linked, as shown, by a rubber-tyred wheel W rolling on a disc D. With a constant speed input the output speed can be varied very easily by moving the driving wheel towards or away from the centre of the rotating disc. This method is often used in the driving mechanism of record and tape players.

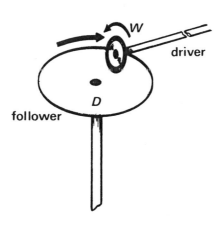

If the radius of D is 5 cm, and the radius of W is 0.5 cm, what is the possible range of transmission factors from W to D?

117

15 A variable speed drive to a potter's wheel is provided
by two rollers *A* and *B* (see below). Roller *A* is in the
shape of a frustum of a cone and is rotated at a constant
speed by an electric motor. Roller *B* is barrel shaped
with a rubberised non-slip surface and one end having
a smaller diameter than the other. The potter can
control the speed of the wheel by moving a lever with
his or her foot, which swings the suspension of *A* so that
different parts of *A* and *B* are in contact.

If *A* turns at 120 rpm and the potter requires the
wheel to turn at speeds varying between 60 rpm and
360 rpm, give possible dimensions for the two rollers.

Design a mechanism to move *A* so that it always keeps
in contact with *B*.

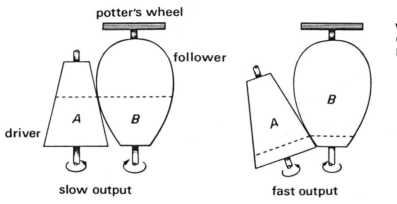

variable speed
drive for a
potter's wheel

16 Investigate the paths
traced out by a point on
the circumference of a
circle as it rolls without
turning (i) inside (ii)
outside a fixed circle.
Such paths are called
hypocycloids and
epicycloids respectively.
They are best
investigated practically
using the Spirograph toy,
but good results can be
achieved using thick card
cut-outs.

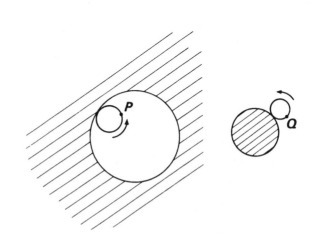

Look particularly at cases where the diameters of the
circles are in a simple ratio to one another.

*17 Two cones with base diameter d and height h are stuck together at their bases to form a roller. The roller is placed on two rails made from card. If the rails are at an angle of elevation of α and at an angle of β to each other, find the condition relating α, β, d and h for the roller to roll in the direction shown, apparently rolling uphill!

Make a model for yourself.

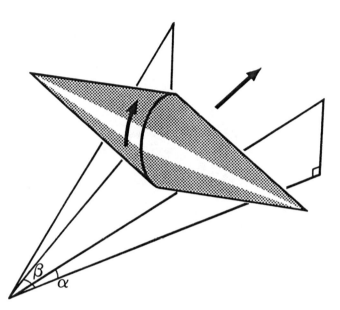

9 Forward twist!

Combining rotary and linear motion

Rotary and linear motion are frequently combined in a mechanism. For example, the mechanism which converts the rotation of a door handle to the withdrawal of the bolt, or the winding drum of a winch which pulls in a rope to lift a weight, or the reciprocating pistons of an engine which turn the flywheel of a car, or the rotation of an electric motor which produces the up and down motion of a sewing machine needle. Sometimes the driver is the rotary element, sometimes the linear motion.

One very important mechanism which is widely used to change rotary motion to linear motion, and vice versa, is the screw.

The screw mechanism

Archimedes (287–212 BC) first wrote about the screw which he saw as an inclined plane wrapped around a cylinder, and this picture gives us a very good approach to understanding this mechanism. Cut out a triangle of paper, as shown, to represent an inclined plane, and wrap it around a cylinder (use a dowel or pencil). The sloping edge of the paper winds its way up the surface of the cylinder at a constant angle of climb α to form a spiral known as a *helix*. Clearly the smaller

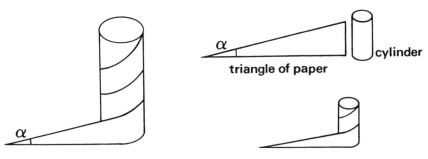

triangle of paper

cylinder

the angle α the more turns of the cylinder will be required to gain the same height.

What is the effect of changing the diameter of the cylinder on the change in height for each turn?

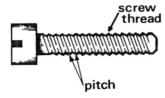

In use, the important thing to know is how far the screw thread will advance along its main axis in completing one revolution, called the *lead*.

When the screw thread consists of a single helix this distance is equal to the distance between adjacent parts of the thread, known as the *pitch*. If, for example, the pitch of a screw is 1 mm, then a nut fitting the screw would have to make 10 complete revolutions to advance 1 cm along its length. Some screws have what are called *multiple start threads*, when the thread consists of more than one helix. This occurs when a screw is designed so that the thread advances rapidly along its length for each revolution.

The figure below illustrates two uses of a screw where it is required to produce a considerable force. The Mini jack is based on a long screw (36 cm) which is turned by a spanner. A nut on the screw is attached to a projecting bar which fits into the chassis of the car and as the screw is turned the nut travels up the screw and lifts the car.

mini jack

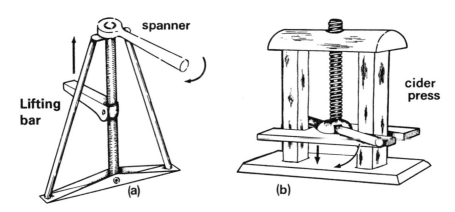

10 complete turns of the screw raises the lifting bar through 4 cm, so the lead is 0.4 cm. If the force is applied to the spanner at a distance of 15 cm from the screw, then the hand applying the force will move through a distance of $2\pi \times 15$ cm for each revolution, giving a transmission factor of

$$\frac{0.4}{30\pi} \simeq \frac{1}{236}$$

If no friction were involved then the work done in turning the spanner would be equal to the work done in lifting the car, so the force required to push the spanner would only be $\frac{1}{236}$ of the force required to lift the car. In practice the frictional force is quite high but even so the transmission factor, which is essentially a spatial concept, gives a good idea of the advantage to be gained.

Cider presses were quite common in country districts where apples were crushed to squeeze out their juice to make cider. They were often on a large scale standing 3 m high, and the large screw would be turned by several men pushing on the long handles to provide a considerable pressure between the two faces of the press.

Like the cider press, but made of metal and on a smaller scale, are the fly presses used for a variety of purposes such as book-binding, printing, embossing coins, and attaching veneers. The fly refers to the weighted cross-piece which is spun like a flywheel to tighten the press.

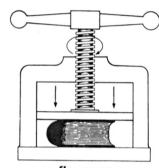

fly press

The uses of a screw mechanism so far discussed have involved ways of increasing the driving force by having a small transmission factor, and similar uses are found in its application to a vice, or a G-clamp. However, many of its uses are concerned with fine adjustments such as the levelling screws on a clock or scientific instrument, or an adjustable glue-stick or lipstick, or for adjusting the height of a music stool or typist's stool, or focusing a camera, or advancing the lead in a propelling pencil.

Normally the screw is turned and the follower moves linearly along the axis of the screw, and the friction is such

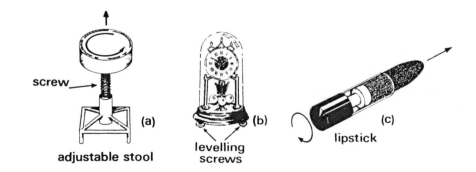

screw

(a)
adjustable stool

(b)
levelling
screws

(c)
lipstick

that the roles of driver and follower could not be reversed.
However small drills and 'Yankee' screwdrivers have been
designed where a 'pumping' action of the nut makes the
screw rotate.

A typical drill of this kind (see below) rotates through 2.4
clockwise revolutions as the nut is pushed through a distance
of 12 cm towards the drill bit, and 2.4 anticlockwise
revolutions as the nut is pulled the 12 cm back to the handle.
The lead of the screw is thus 12 cm ÷ 2.4 = 5 cm. Careful
inspection also showed that this drill had a 4-start screw as
it had 4 'parallel' threads.

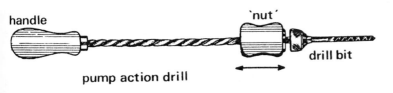

pump action drill

Archimedean screw

One of the famous mechanisms of the ancients is the
Archimedian screw which was designed by Archimedes for
drawing water from a river to irrigate the land.

The thread of the screw is like a continuously curving blade
in the shape of a helix which fits closely inside a cylindrical
pipe so that, as it turns, water at one end of the pipe is drawn
along the pipe by the screw. A modern use of the mechanism
is seen in many kitchens in the meat mincer, but it is also
used commercially to move liquids and grain around
processing plants.

A wood drill is not unlike an Archimedean screw. At one
end it has a small diameter tapered screw which pulls the
main drill with its cutting edge slowly through the wood,
while behind the cutting edge an Archimedean screw
systematically removes the cut wood from the hole.

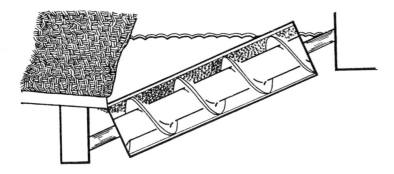

The three blades of the ship's propeller shown here are rather like parts of a 3-start screw and as they turn they effectively screw their way through the water on helical paths. A high speed propeller has blades which are almost at right angles to the axis so that the pitch of the screw is relatively small. This type of propeller would be found on an outboard motor, in contrast to the propellers on a large tanker which turn relatively slowly and are at a significant angle, giving a longer pitch. In practice 'slippage' occurs so that the propellers only move forward relative to the water at about 70% of the distance the pitch would indicate.

Over the years engineers have developed variable pitch propellers for varying conditions for ships, planes and helicopters.

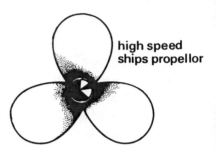

high speed
ships propellor

The rack and pinion

Rack and pinion gearing consists of a normal gear wheel, the *pinion*, which meshes with a straight toothed bar, the *rack*. If, as in (a), the pinion rotates about a fixed axis, then the rack moves sideways. But if the rack is fixed as in (b), then the pinion moves sideways as it rotates. In practice the rack and pinion mechanism is used in both these modes.

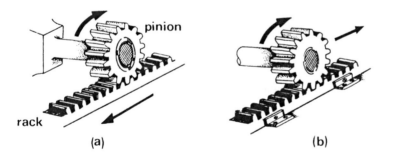

pinion

rack

(a)   (b)

With the pinion fixed it can easily be used as a mechanism for bolting a door, where the door knob is connected to the pinion, and the rack is an extension of the bolt.

Anyone who has been on a canal holiday and spent time and energy turning the handles at the locks, which raise the paddles to release the water, should recognise this mechanism, for the control rod from the paddle ends in a rack driven by a pinion connected directly to the handle being turned.

Most car steering mechanisms employ the rack and pinion gear. The steering column ends in a small pinion which engages in a rack forming part of the track rod of an Ackermann steering mechanism (see page 71) so that turning the steering wheel pushes the track rod sideways and changes the angles of the front wheels.

In the fifteenth century Leonardo da Vinci showed how a rack and pinion, suitably geared, could be used in the design of a jack to lift heavy weights. In the jack illustrated the handle A is connected to the gear B with 6 teeth. Gear B meshes with gear C which has 14 teeth and this in turn meshes with a vertical rack D, which raises the load. So for every revolution of the handle the rack moves up 6 teeth. The transmission factor will depend on the length of the handle and the distance between the teeth on the rack. If, for example, the handle is 20 cm long and the distance between the teeth is 0.5 cm then in one revolution the handle A will move through $2\pi \times 20$ cm and the rack will rise through 6×0.5 cm giving a transmission factor of

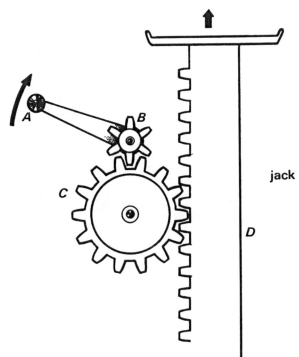

jack

$$\frac{6 \times 0.5}{2\pi \times 20} \simeq \frac{1}{42}$$

so, ignoring friction, the jack should be able to raise a load 42 times as large as the force applied to the handle.

Jacks similar to this were widely used in Britain and the USA from the end of the eighteenth century.

A classic use of the rack and pinion mechanism is its application to mountain railways such as the railway which climbs to the top of Snowdon. Because of the steep gradients up Snowdon, a climb of over 1000 metres in under 8 kilometres, the usual driving wheels of an engine would slip on the rails. To overcome this a rack is introduced midway between the rails, and a toothed driving wheel in the engine engages with the teeth in the rack, enabling the train to progress without any slipping.

In this use of the mechanism the rack is stationary and the pinion rolls along it without slipping. A similar use, but on a much smaller scale, can be found on scientific instruments such as microscopes or photographic enlargers, where a turn of a knob linked to the pinion moves part of the instrument along a rack for careful focusing or other purpose. See what examples you can find of its use in this mode.

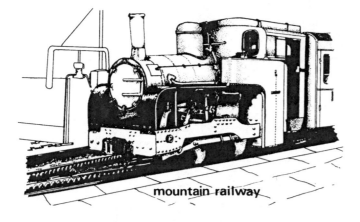

mountain railway

Door locks

Door locks come in many shapes and sizes but apart from a simple bolt which is pushed sideways into position, most are operated by turning a handle and/or a key to move the bolt.

Dismantling a lock is quite enlightening. The basic mechanism of one is shown below. A spring normally pushes

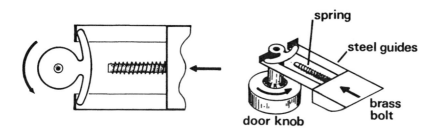

spring

steel guides

brass bolt

door knob

the brass bolt to the right. The bolt is attached to two steel guides which end in two raised flanges at right-angles to the guides. The door knob is attached to two projecting levers, one of which pulls the bolt into the lock as the knob is turned by pushing against the raised end of one of the guides. The two levers ensure that whichever way the door knob is turned, the bolt will be drawn into the lock.

The figure below shows the mechanism in a typical back door lock which is operated by a key. In this case the brass bolt is attached to a flat steel plate which contains three holes. Two of these are guide holes which slide on two pins in the casing of the lock, while the large hole is shaped to allow the key bit to engage its rim and push it sideways as the key is turned. The symmetry of the hole in the sliding plate allows the key to work no matter which way up it is inserted into the lock. In this case no spring is involved and the direction in which the bolt is moved will depend on the direction of rotation of the key.

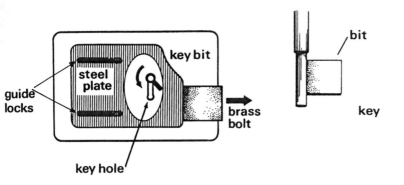

The distance moved by the bolt of a lock for a given angle of turn of the door knob or key is a significant part of the design of the locking mechanism, and in the designs shown it depends to a large extent on the lengths of the levers and key bit.

Other designs are discussed in the exercise, but many interesting locking mechanisms can be found for securing the lids of old treasure chests, which can be seen in museums and churches.

Further, the design of keys and tumblers for a Yale type lock is a study in itself, but not the main point of this chapter.

Exercise 9

1   Investigate the *lead* (distance moved linearly for one revolution) of the screws in as many of the following mechanisms that you can find:
    (a) a glue-stick,
    (b) a lipstick,
    (c) a propelling pencil,
    (d) a screw jack,
    (e) a vice,
    (f) a screw clamp,
    (g) a typist's stool,
    (h) a cold water tap,
    (i) a wood drill,
    (j) a meat mincer,
    (k) a nut and bolt,
    (l) a Yankee screw driver,
    (m) a wood screw,
    (n) a Black and Decker or similar work bench,
    (o) the rear sight on a rifle,
    (p) the screw lid on a coffee jar,
    (q) a micrometer screw gauge,
    (r) a corkscrew,
    (s) a cider press,
    (t) an adjustable spanner,
    (u) screw type nut crackers.
       Also try to find whether or not the screws are single or multiple threaded.

2   There are many kinds of screw jack designed with different purposes in mind, from lifting small cars to traction engines, or for holding a beam in place while a builder does repairs. Try to locate a variety of screw jacks and find out their transmission factors in each case. Check this against the kind of load they are designed to lift. It should be the case that the larger the design load the smaller the transmission factor.

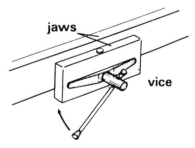

double lift jack

3   A bench vice has two jaws which are pulled together by a screw with a thread whose pitch is 0.4 cm by pushing the handle whose length is 12 cm.
       What is the transmission factor?

jaws

vice

128

How could the transmission factor be made even smaller?

4 The handle of a G-clamp is 7 cm long. 20 revolutions of the handle open the jaws of the clamp a distance of 3.6 cm. What is the transmission factor for the clamp?

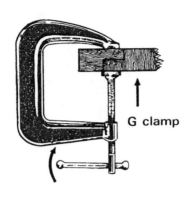

G clamp

If a force of 5 kg weight is applied to the end of the handle and no friction is involved, what would be the force between the jaws of the clamp?

5 The figure below shows a typical adjustable wrench. The screw is turned using a finger tip to adjust the distance between the jaws of the wrench and not to apply pressure between them. In one such wrench the diameter of the screw is 1.5 cm and 6 revolutions of the screw will open or close the jaws of the wrench 3.4 cm. Find the transmission factor of this wrench and compare it with other similar ones you come across.

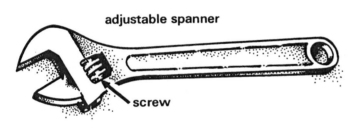

adjustable spanner

screw

6 A jack is designed around a rack and pinion mechanism as shown in the figure. The handle AB is of length 16 cm and turns a gear wheel at B with 9 teeth. This gear meshes with gear wheel C having 36 teeth. Gear wheel D with 4 teeth turns together with C and engages the teeth on the rack, E. The distance between the teeth on the rack is 0.6 cm.

Find the vertical distance moved by the rack for one turn of the handle and calculate the transmission factor for the jack.

If 50% of the work done in lifting a load using the jack is to overcome the frictional forces in the mechanism, what force is required at A to lift a load of 500 kg?

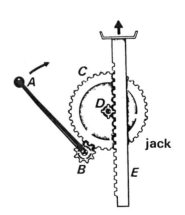

jack

7 The feed for an electric drill consists of a vertical rack and a pinion which is turned by the operator pulling on a 3-pronged handle.

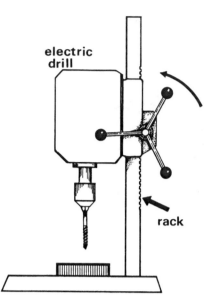

If the handle's length is 18 cm, the pinion has 8 teeth, and the distance between the teeth on the rack is 0.2 cm, find the transmission factor. Given that the mechanism is 70% efficient, what force will be applied at the tip of the drill when the operator pulls the handle with a force of 5 kg wt?

8 Use a Lego Technic or Fischertechnik or Meccano kit to make a model employing a rack and pinion mechanism.

9 Design a door fastening mechanism based on a rack and pinion so that a 180° rotation of the door handle moves the bolt 2 cm.

10 A door locking mechanism is based on the *scotch yoke* mechanism (see below). As the disc is turned, by turning the door knob, a pin on the disc engages in the slot in the slide.

Describe the motion of the bolt as the disc makes one revolution.

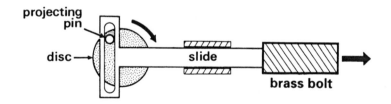

What determines the throw of the bolt?

11 Many modern door locking mechanisms are designed so that as the door handle is turned 3 bolts are pushed into place: one into the door frame at the side, one to the top, and one to the bottom. Design a mechanism to do this.

10 A bumpy ride!

Cams and ratchets

Cams are specially shaped objects designed to drive a follower in a specific way. The two examples shown are typical of rotating cams whose radius varies from the axis of rotation, and hence each drive their vertical rod in a reciprocating motion. But the motions of the rods will differ considerably. In figure (a) the cam has essentially two different but constant radii, so for most of the time the vertical rod will be at one of two heights. In figure (b) however the radius is continuously changing and the rod moves up and down in a harmonic fashion.

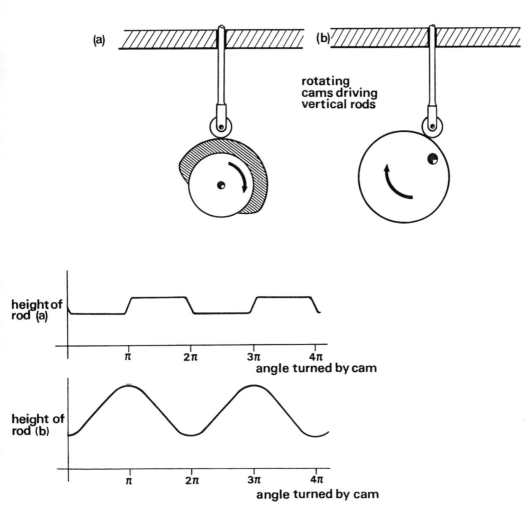

(a)   (b)

rotating cams driving vertical rods

height of rod (a)

π   2π   3π   4π
angle turned by cam

height of rod (b)

π   2π   3π   4π
angle turned by cam

The graphs show the behaviour of the rods for two revolutions of each cam, starting with the rod at its lowest position in each case.

131

From these two examples alone, something of the potential of the cam mechanism can be appreciated, so it is not surprising to find that some authors claim it to be the most versatile of all mechanisms.

One of the most common uses of cams is in the mechanism for opening the valves of a car engine. Each cylinder of a petrol engine has two valves, one for letting the mixture of petrol and air in and another for letting the exhaust gases out. So a typical 4-cylinder car engine has 8 valves and these are operated by 8 cams, all mounted on the same shaft geared to the engine's crankshaft so as to open the valves at just the right point in the combustion cycle.

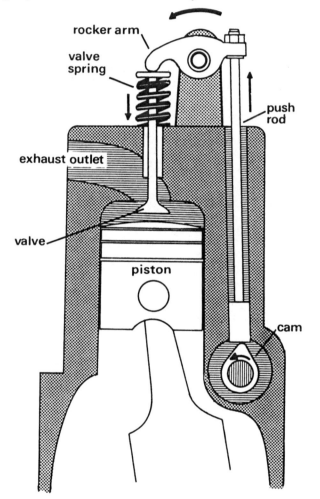

The figure above shows a typical arrangement. As the cam turns, the projecting portion of the cam will push the push rod upwards, which in turn will rotate the rocker arm and push the valve downwards against the spring, allowing the exhaust gases to escape. When the valve is not being forced down by the rocker arm the valve spring forces it up into the closed position.

In some engines, with an overhead camshaft, the cams operate directly on the top of the valves, while in others, because of the positions of the valves in the cylinder, the inlet valves are driven directly by cams, but the exhaust valves require rocker arms to transmit the cams' motion. Clearly the distance moved by the valve in opening, and the time for which it is open, will depend on the design of the cam and position of the pivot in the rocker arm, which can be used to increase or decrease the movement the cam produces in the push rod.

An ingenious use of a cam is seen on traditional sewing machines as part of the mechanism to feed cotton evenly onto a spool when it is being rewound (see figure). As the spool rotates at constant speed the cotton guide must move to and fro across the spool at a constant speed. This is achieved by the cam B which is geared to the spool's drive shaft using a worm gear engaging a spur gear, as shown. The cotton guide is pivoted at A and a spring ensures that it keeps in contact with the cam. The number of teeth on the spur gear determines the number of revolutions of the spool as the cotton guide moves once from right to left and back again. One such mechanism I examined had 144 teeth on the spur gear, so there will be 72 winds of cotton across the width of the spool.

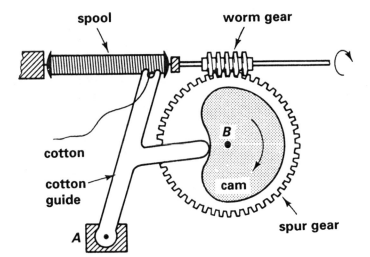

Another use of a cam is in the mechanism of a musical box. Here a rotating drum has tiny pins projecting from it which pluck metal reeds as the drum turns. By suitably placing the pins, the drums can pluck the reeds in any sequence required and hence represent any tune. Because the drum has to rotate slowly it is usually driven through a worm and spur gear train.

musical box
mechanism

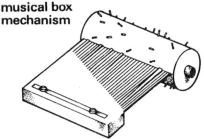

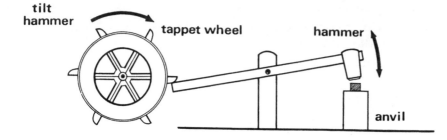

Very similar to the musical box, but on a much larger scale, is the mechanism shown for a tilt hammer. A heavy hammer is pivoted so that its head rests on an anvil. The other end of the hammer's shaft is then periodically pushed and released by the projections of a rotating tappet wheel which is in effect a cam. Such hammers were widely used in foundries from the beginning of the industrial revolution and were usually powered by waterwheels. A good example can still be seen at Finch's Foundry in Sticklepath, Devon.

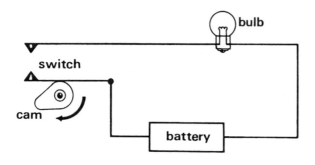

Rotary switches are often designed to be operated by a cam and are particularly useful where a sequence of *on* and *off* has to be repeated over and over again. With the circuit above the bulb will light when the cam turns and closes the switch contacts, but will go out as soon as the cam moves to a position where the switch contacts no longer meet. The ratio of the time when the bulb is alight to not alight can be determined by the raised portion of the cam, and a sequence of flashes could easily be arranged. For example, two short flashes followed by a long flash would be produced by a rotary switch with the cam shown above.

It is not difficult to see how cams could be designed to produce the sequence of flashes for a particular lighthouse, or an advertising display, or fairground lights, or a set of traffic lights.

Some cars use electronic ignition but many engines rely on a rotating cam to control the switch which sends power to the sparking plugs at the right time. The cam is almost square in cross section and makes and breaks the circuit four times in each revolution, once for each cylinder of the engine.

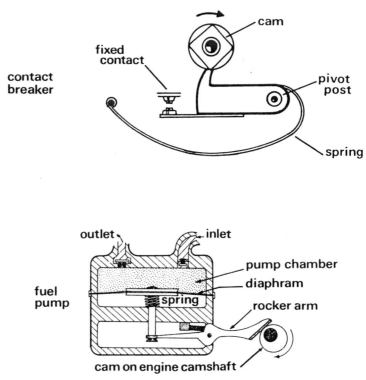

A circular off-centre cam, known as an *eccentric cam*, is used to drive the mechanical fuel pump on many cars (see figure). It pushes a rocker arm which pulls down a flexible diaphragm to suck petrol into the pump chamber. Then, as the cam turns, the diaphragm is pushed up by a spring forcing petrol through the outlet valve to the carburettor. carburettor.

The cams considered so far have all been two-dimensional in concept, but the two shown below are essentially three-dimensional.

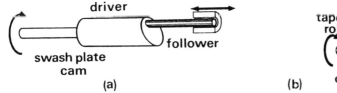

(a)

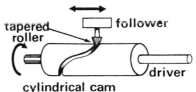

(b)

The swash plate cam uses the flat face of a cylinder cut at an angle to its axis of symmetry to impart a reciprocating motion to a rod in the direction of its axis. Such a mechanism is used to drive the pumps in the hydraulic systems for operating modern aircraft.

The cylindrical cam has a helical groove in its surface and a small tapered roller inserted in the groove is fixed to a follower which is free to move in the direction of the axis of the cylinder. The result is that the follower is translated as the cylinder turns. This positive motion cam, which does not require a spring or gravity to keep the follower in contact, is used in the textile industry, and in the steering mechanism of some cars in place of a rack and pinion mechanism.

The mechanism in some lawn mowers which allows the blades to go on spinning when the driving wheels stop turning is quite ingenious and is shown below. The cam in this case might be called a ring cam. As the mower is pushed from left to right the driving wheel turns clockwise and one of its three protruding lugs will engage with the sliding bar of the follower, which is geared to turn the cutting blades. But if the mower stops or is pulled backwards, the shape of the cam pushes the sliding bar to and fro so that it does not engage with the driver.

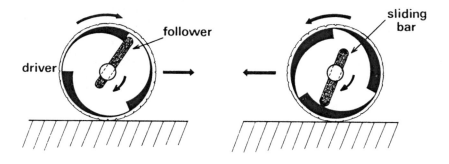

In general, cams have very wide applicability, for by a suitable design almost any pattern of motion can be achieved from a constant speed input. In particular, it is possible to achieve pauses in the motion of any length, a feature not easily obtainable using other mechanisms, or to produce precisely controlled movements such as required in guiding a milling cutter.

Not discussed here, but of importance in practice, is the analysis of the speed and acceleration of the follower for different shaped cams.

The rear brakes of most cars are drum brakes. Two metal brake shoes X and Y, covered with special linings to withstand heat, are pivoted at P and pushed outwards against the rotating brake drum when the brake is applied. The way in which the shoes are operated varies, but one method used is that of a brake lever linked to a cam as shown on the right. This is particularly applicable where a brake pedal or hand brake is linked to the brake drums by a wire. The hydraulic solution is discussed on page 151.

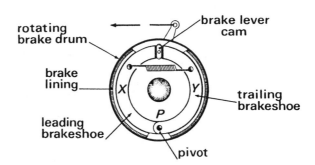

Only one way

A number of mechanisms are designed to allow movement in one direction but to prevent movement in the opposite direction. The most common such mechanism is the *ratchet and pawl* which occurs in the free wheel of a bicycle or the winding mechanism of a traditional watch or clock.

Figures (a) and (b) show the basic mechanism. In (a) the ratchet bar is free to slide to the left, but can move at most the distance between consecutive teeth of the ratchet bar to the right before being stopped by the pawl, which is sprung to keep in contact with the bar. Similarly the ratchet wheel, (b), is free to turn in an anticlockwise direction but would not be able to turn very far in a clockwise direction before being stopped by the pawl. To allow the movement in the reverse direction the pawl must be held away from the ratchet teeth.

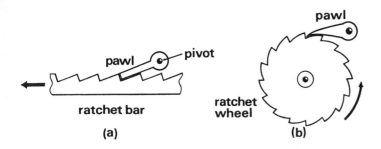

When releasing the handbrake of a car, for example, the driver first pulls the brake further on to release the force on the pawl, and then presses the button on the top of the lever which disengages the pawl from the ratchet track.

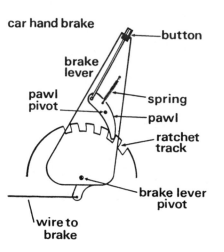

car hand brake

Most winding mechanisms contain a ratchet and pawl so that when the person doing the winding stops applying a force, the load being wound in does not immediately unwind, but is held at the point reached. The clicking noise you hear as you wind a watch or fishing reel, or the tick, tick, tick, you hear in the free wheel of a bicycle, is the sound of the pawls jumping over the ratchet teeth when the ratchet wheel is moving relative to the pawl.

The free wheel of a bicycle has the ratchet teeth protruding on the inside, while the pawls which are sprung to engage it are pivoted to an inner ring which is fixed to turn with the rear wheel. When the cyclist is pedalling the pawls engage the ratchet in the free wheel so that the rear wheel of the cycle turns at the same speed as the free wheel, but as soon as the cyclist stops pedalling the free wheel becomes stationary and the inner ring continues to turn with the rear wheel, allowing the pawls to bounce over the ratchet teeth, giving their familiar tune.

A traditional cart jack which used to be made by the village blacksmith, has a simple application of the ratchet and pawl mechanism, as well as illustrating the use of a lever and a parallelogram linkage.

A modern version of such a jack can often be found in use in garages.

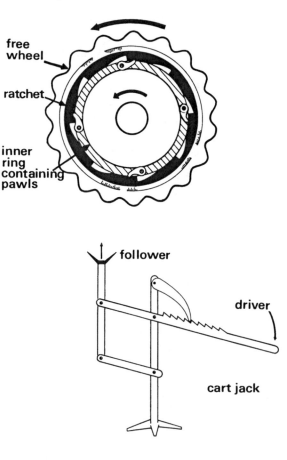

138

There are many manufacturing processes where it is useful to move a conveyor belt, or object to be operated on, in discrete steps. One way to do this is to use the pawl to drive the ratchet. If the pivot of the pawl, A in figure, is driven on a circular path, then the pawl will push the slide in such a way that it will be stationary for half the time, and be pushed a distance equivalent to one tooth of the ratchet for each revolution of the driver.

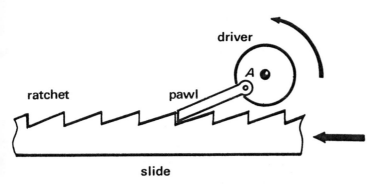

An interesting application of the ratchet and pawl mechanism was described by Polhelm early in the eighteenth century to operate a winch. The figure below shows its main features. A winding drum D is on the same shaft as a ratchet wheel which is prevented from unwinding by the pawl pivoted at R. To wind the winch a lever pivoted at P is moved up and down. Pivoted on the lever at Q is a second pawl which engages a tooth of the ratchet wheel on each down stroke and moves it on one tooth. The transmission factor is thus very small but will enable large loads to be lifted.

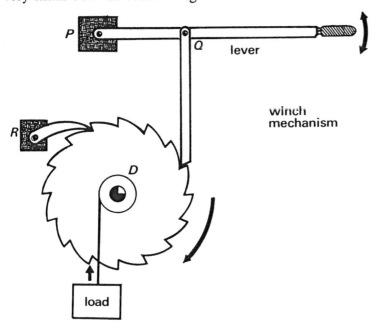

A not dissimilar mechanism is the escapement mechanism of a clock or watch (see figure). A ratchet wheel known as the escape wheel is being driven clockwise by weights (as in a grandfather clock) or a spring (as in a carriage clock) but its motion is impeded by the pawls B and C, known as pallets, on the anchor which oscillates to and fro about the pivot A. In the position shown the escape wheel is about to push the pawl C to the right but in doing so pawl B will move down to engage the teeth of the escape wheel. Next, the escape wheel will push pawl B out of its way and rock the anchor until pawl C engages the teeth of the escape wheel,

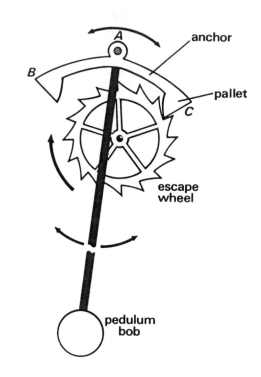

and so on. The rate at which the anchor rocks controls the speed at which the escape wheel can turn, and this is determined by attaching the anchor to a pendulum whose period of oscillation depends on the distance of the bob from the pivot A. In a grandfather clock this is adjusted so that the pendulum makes a complete oscillation (over and back) in exactly 2 seconds. The escape wheel hence moves forward one tooth every 2 seconds and by gearing the hands of the clock to the shaft carrying the escape wheel the clock will keep the correct time.

Exercise 10

1   The figure shows a cam driving a pointed follower which is free to move up and down. Such followers are used where abrupt changes in the cam's contour occurs.

  Assuming that the largest radius of the cam is twice the smallest radius, draw a graph to

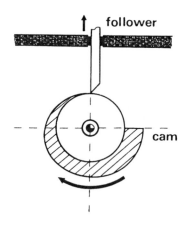

show the displacement of the follower for 2 complete revolutions of the cam.

2   The mechanism in question 1 has its cam replaced in turn by the three cams shown below. Draw the graph to show the displacement of the follower for 2 complete revolutions of the cam in each case. Could the cams be used if they were rotated anticlockwise?

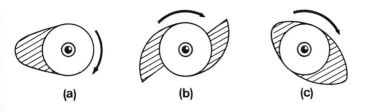

(a)   (b)   (c)

3   A circular eccentric cam rotates about A inside a rectangular yoke fixed to a sliding follower. If the smallest radius of the cam is p and its largest radius is q, what are the internal dimensions of the yoke assuming the cam touches all its sides during one revolution? What are the limits of the displacement of the follower?

Draw a graph of the follower's displacement, from its middle position with the cam upwards, against the angle turned by the cam.

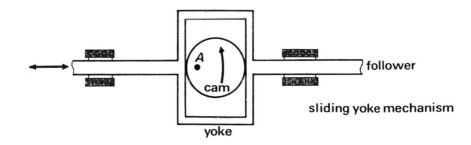

follower

sliding yoke mechanism

yoke

4   Design a sliding yoke mechanism so that the distance between the extreme points of the motion is 2 cm. Given that the motor available turns at a speed of 240 rpm and the yoke is required to make 30 complete (to and fro) strokes per minute, design a suitable gear train to drive the cam.

5 The graphs below each give the vertical displacement z of a pointed follower driven by a cam turning about a horizontal shaft. Make a drawing of a suitable cam in each case.

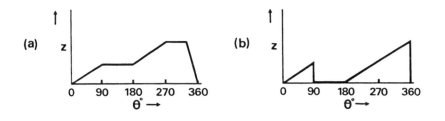

6 In a lighting display one set of lights is designed to come on for 20 seconds, be off for 20 seconds, be on for 10 seconds, and then off for 10 seconds in every minute.

Design a cam driven rotary switch to operate the lights.

7 Analyse the timing sequence for the red, green, and amber lights of a set of traffic lights known to you, and hence design a suitable cam driven set of rotary switches which could be used to operate them.

8 How does a chiming clock know when to chime?

9 A record for a record player is a glorified cam. Explain this statement.

10 Investigate the ratchet mechanism in
   (a) a fishing reel;
   (b) a telephone dial;
   (c) a winch;
   (d) a car's hand brake;
   (e) a ratchet screwdriver;
   (f) a ratchet drill;
   (g) a cycle free wheel.

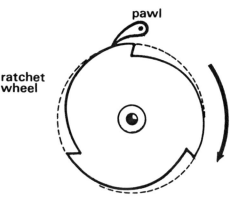

11 The ratchet wheel shown has three equally spaced teeth. The single pawl is sprung towards the wheel.
   (a) What is the largest angle through which the wheel could turn

clockwise before being stopped by the pawl?

(b) How many teeth would need to be added to the wheel to reduce the maximum angle through which the wheel could turn clockwise to 60°?

(c) By adding a further pawl to the mechanism shown it is also possible to reduce the maximum clockwise angle. Explain.

12 Investigate the escapement mechanism on a pendulum clock. Time the period of oscillation of the pendulum, by timing 20 oscillations. Now count the number of teeth on the escape wheel and determine the time for it to make one revolution. Next see how the minute and hour hands are geared to the escape wheel to keep the correct time.

13 The figure below shows two mechanisms which will allow a belt to travel in one direction but not the other. Describe how they work and in which way the belt would be free to travel in each case.

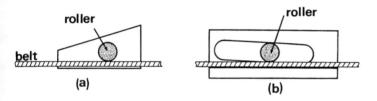

14 How do inertia reel car seat belts operate?

15 Many gate and door fastenings allow the gate or door to close but then do not permit further movement. See how many different such mechanisms you can find and analyse the underlying principles of the mechanisms.

11 Win some, lose some!

Levers and hydraulic rams

Levers

When a rigid rod AB is free to turn about a fixed pivot O, then it effectively becomes a lever. If $AO = a$ and $BO = b$ then if the rod turns through an angle θ, the ends of the rod travel along arcs of circles of length $a\theta$ and $b\theta$ respectively (see below). Hence the ratio of the distances moved by A and B is proportional to their distances from the pivot O, namely $a{:}b$.

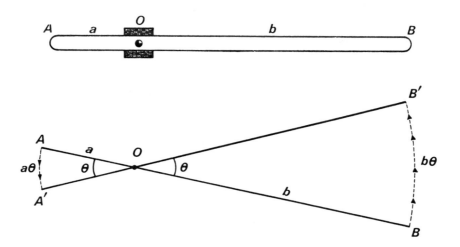

The use of a simple lever to move heavy objects has been a known technique for as long as records have been kept. The following figure shows a man pushing down on one end of a long bar, which pivots on a stone at O, to lift the large boulder at A. The work done by the man in pushing the bar down at B will be equal to the work done on the boulder at A, due to a fundamental law of physics. But the work done by a force is equal to the product of the force and the distance it moves, so

$$\begin{array}{cc}\text{force} \times \text{distance moved} = \text{force} \times \text{distance moved}\\ \text{at } B \qquad\qquad \text{by } B \qquad\qquad \text{at } A \qquad\qquad \text{by } A\end{array}$$

from which

$$\frac{\text{force at } B}{\text{force at } A} = \frac{\text{distance moved by } A}{\text{distance moved by } B} = \frac{a}{b}$$

which is in effect the transmission factor of A relative to B.

144

If, for example, $a = 0.5$ cm, and $b = 3.0$ m, then $a/b = \frac{1}{6}$, so a man pushing down with a force of 40 kg wt at B would be able to lift a load of $6 \times 40 = 240$ kg wt at A. By moving the pivot closer to the boulder so that $a/b = \frac{1}{20}$ say, then the same 40 kg wt force at B would enable the man to apply a force of 800 kg wt to the boulder. But it would need B to move down 20 cm to raise A through 1 cm.

Levers are frequently classified into 3 types, depending on the relative positions of the pivot, the applied force, and the load on the lever.

The figure below shows this classification. In each case P is the applied force at B and Q gives the load which can be balanced at A by the lever pivoted at O, where

$$\frac{P}{Q} = \frac{OA}{OB}$$

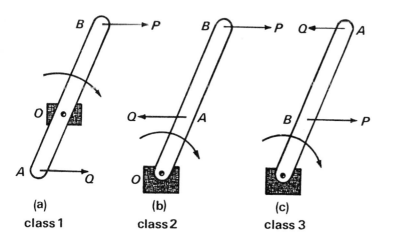

(a)	(b)	(c)
class 1	class 2	class 3

145

The foot pedals in a car are all examples of class 2 levers, while the hand brake is a class 1 lever. The small movements of a person standing on bathroom scales are magnified by the use of class 3 levers, as are the pointers and pen arms of aneroid barometers and barographs.

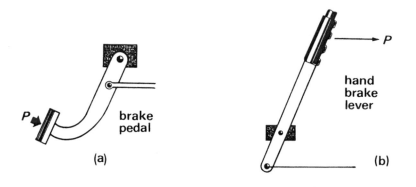

(a)

(b)

Levers are often used in pairs as in pairs of scissors, or grass shears, or nutcrackers or pliers. Why is it easier to cut something near to the pivot than near to the tips of a pair of scissors? What class of lever is normally used in nutcrackers?

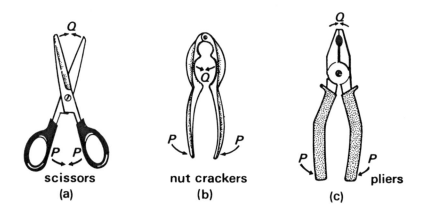

A good example of a class 2 lever is a capstan winch. Each of the 'arms' of the capstan is a lever pivoted about its end, which coincides with the axis of the winch. A force is applied to the outside end of each arm to turn the capstan and produce a force Q in the rope. The longer the arms of the capstan relative to the radius of the winding drum, the further the applied forces P will travel relative to the distance moved by the rope, and consequently the larger the load Q which can be pulled in. Note the ratchet and pawl mechanism at the base of the capstan to stop it slipping back.

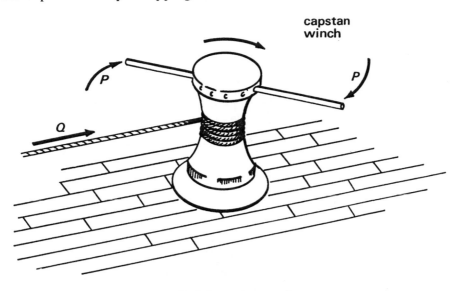

capstan winch

Often situations occur where an applied force has to be turned through an angle and this can neatly be effected by a 'bent' lever known as a *bell crank*. These were much in evidence in the traditional railway signalling system, which had signal boxes full of levers linked to remote signals and points by wires and rods joined together by bell cranks. But a familiar use to most readers will be the caliper brakes on a bicycle, where the brake cable pulls two levers together vertically, but their ends holding the brake blocks move horizontally. Long handled garden shears for trimming the edges of lawns also employ bent levers.

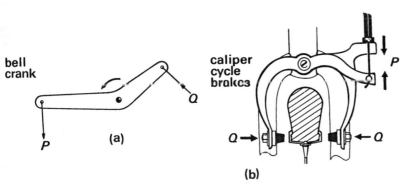

bell crank

(a)

caliper cycle brakes

(b)

The following figure shows a traditional cheese press which uses a combination of a simple pulley system and levers to press a cheese. To find how the effect of the weight at A is multiplied by the time it reaches the press it is necessary to find how far G moves compared to A.

147

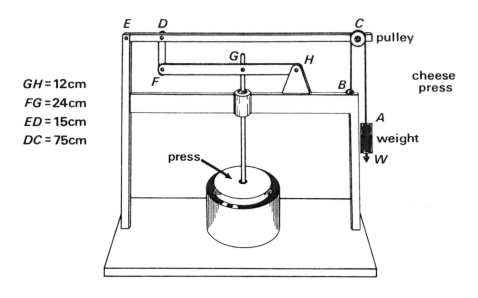

GH = 12cm
FG = 24cm
ED = 15cm
DC = 75cm

Suppose *G* moves down 1 cm, then as *FH* = 36 cm, and *GH* = 12 cm, it follows that *FH* = 3*GH* so *F* moves down 3 cm.

Now *EC* = 90 cm, and *ED* = 15 cm, so *EC* = 6*ED*, hence *C* moves down 6 × 3 cm = 18 cm. But the weight *A* will move down twice as far as the pulley *C*, so *A* moves down 36 cm. Hence the transmission factor of *A* relative to *G* is 36.

So, ignoring any loss due to frictional forces, the force on the cheese due to the weight *W* at *A* will be 36*W*.

Simple hydraulics

The French mathematician Blaise Pascal (1623–62) was the first person to make explicit the principle on which many mechanisms depend. Consider the apparatus below which consists of two pistons sliding in cylinders connected by a tube. The shaded regions represent a fluid, which for our purposes can be assumed to have a constant volume. So as piston *A* is pushed to the right, the volume of fluid squeezed out of the large cylinder enters the small cylinder and pushes piston *B* to the right. If the cross-sectional area of piston *A*

is k times the cross-sectional area of piston B, then piston B will move k times as far as piston A for the volume to remain constant.

Suppose, for example, piston A has a cross-sectional area of 20 cm² and piston B a cross-sectional area of 5 cm². If piston A moves 2 cm to the right it will squeeze $2 \times 20 = 40$ cm³ of fluid into cylinder B, so piston B will have to move $40 \div 5 = 8$ cm to the right to make room for the increase in fluid.

In general then

$$\frac{\text{distance moved by } B}{\text{distance moved by } A} = \frac{\text{cross-sectional area of } A}{\text{cross-sectional area of } B}$$

Now if A is pushed with a force P and B exerts a force Q, as with the lever, the work done on A is equal to the work done by B, so

$$P \times \text{distance moved by } A = Q \times \text{distance moved by } B$$

from which

$$\frac{P}{Q} = \frac{\text{distance moved by } B}{\text{distance moved by } A}$$

and from the above equation it follows that

$$\boxed{\frac{P}{Q} = \frac{\text{cross-sectional area of } A}{\text{cross-sectional area of } B}}$$

Pascal demonstrated this basic concept in 1647 with an apparatus consisting of a tank of water with a lid which included two open cylinders of significantly different cross-sectional areas, in which sat two pistons. By placing weights on the pistons proportional to their cross-sectional areas he obtained a hydrostatic balance. But it was not until 1795 that the British engineer Joseph Bramah saw the practical possibilities of the principle and patented a *hydraulic press*.

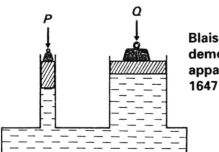

Blaise Pascals's demonstration apparatus 1647

By using a small piston moving a long way, hydraulically linked to a piston with a much larger area, a small force can be used to produce a very large force. By 1799 Bramah had designed a press which produced a force equivalent to 400 tonnes and in a very short time these presses became widely used for such varied jobs as packing raw cotton into dense bales, squeezing oil out of nuts, printing patterns onto cloth, and pressing steel ingots into required shapes. One problem you will have recognised is that when the ratio of the areas of the pistons is very large, the small piston would need to travel a very long way to obtain any significant movement of the large piston. This has been overcome in a number of ways.

hydraulic press

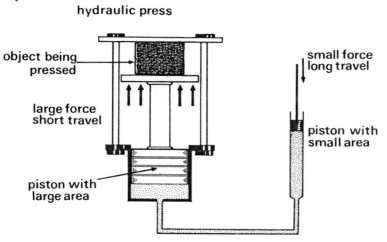

The hydraulic bottle jack for DIY motorists, capable of lifting 1.5 tonnes, is one solution which combines the advantage of a lever with a hydraulic mechanism. Two pistons A and B, known as *rams*, slide in closely fitting cylinders which are interconnected and sit inside a sealed container of fluid. When the handle is pushed down, the small ram A pushes the fluid in its cylinder through the delivery passage, via the non-return valve V_1 into the cylinder B which has a relatively large cross-section. The effect is to raise the ram B by a small amount. Note that as ram A descends it sucks in fluid from the reservoir through the hole X, to fill the volume it has displaced, while ram B will rise and push an identical volume of fluid through hole Y to keep the volume of fluid in the reservoir constant.

When the handle is raised, ram A draws in fluid from the reservoir through V_1 to keep the pressure chamber full of fluid, so that when ram A is again pushed down, another small volume of fluid is forced through V_1 into cylinder B. Hence moving the handle up and down 20 times is equivalent to moving ram A along a cylinder 20 times the length of cylinder A.

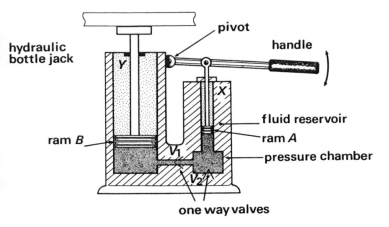

hydraulic
bottle jack

pivot

handle

Y

X

fluid reservoir

ram B

ram A

V_1

pressure chamber

V_2

one way valves

Suppose the cross-sectional area of B is 100 times the cross-sectional area of A, and suppose the distance of the handle from the pivot is 5 times the distance of the ram from the pivot. Then the handle will move 5 times as far as ram A, while ram A will move 100 times as far as ram B, so the transmission factor from the handle to ram B will be $\frac{1}{500}$. This in turn means that the force available at the lifting ram B will be 500 times the force applied to the handle!

Braking systems on cars and motor cycles invariably make use of hydraulics to transmit the force applied at the brake pedal to the brake pads, whether they are disc brakes or drum brakes. When a person presses the brake pedal (figure (a)) the effect is to push a hydraulic ram along the master cylinder, which forces the brake fluid along metal pipes or pressure hoses to the rams operating the brakes. The front brakes are usually disc brakes (figure (b)) and consist of a pair of brake pads squeezed against the surface of a metal

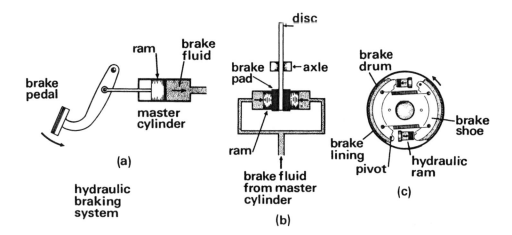

disc

ram

brake
fluid

brake
pad — axle

brake
drum

brake
pedal

master
cylinder

ram

brake
lining

pivot

brake
shoe

hydraulic
ram

(a)

brake fluid
from master
cylinder

(c)

hydraulic
braking
system

(b)

disc which rotates with the front wheel. But unlike the caliper brakes of a bicycle, the squeeze is produced by two hydraulic rams activated by the brake fluid being forced from the master cylinder.

The rear brakes are normally drum brakes (figure (c)), and the two brake shoes are pressed out against the brake drums by another pair of hydraulic rams activated by the brake fluid from the master cylinder.

Suppose the master cylinder and the 8 hydraulic rams (2 for each wheel) had the same cross-section. Then whatever volume of fluid was pushed out of the master cylinder would have to be shared between 8 hydraulic rams at the brakes. So these rams would only move $\frac{1}{8}$ of the distance of the ram in the master cylinder. It follows that the force produced in the rams at the brakes will be 8 times as large as the force with which the ram is pushed along the master cylinder. But the brakes will need to be carefully adjusted, for the travel of the brake rams will be small compared to the travel of the brake pedal, particularly when the effect of the lever to which the brake pedal is attached is also taken into account.

Modern hydraulic systems based on rams with a long travel, as seen on JCBs, tractors, cranes, or aircraft to operate control surfaces, or on industrial robots, all make use of pumps to force the hydraulic fluid from one side of a ram to the other under pressure.

In the figure below a hydraulic pump extracts fluid from B and pushes fluid into A with the result that the ram is pushed to the right. If the direction of rotation of the pump is reversed, then the ram will move to the left.

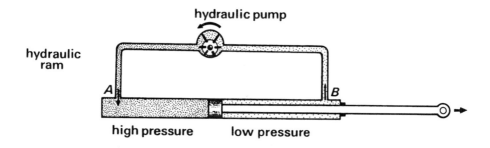

Hydraulic pumps are designed to produce a significant pressure difference in the fluid each side of the ram. Suppose a pump can produce a pressure differential of 12 kg wt per cm² and the cross-sectional area of the ram is 60 cm², then the ram will be pushed with a force of 720 kg wt. How fast it will move then depends on the volume of fluid which passes through the pump per second. For example, if it was 120 cm³/s then the ram would be moved at 2 cm/s.

The gear pump consists of two gears meshed together in a closely fitting casing. The hydraulic fluid (usually oil) is captured between the gear teeth and casing at *A* and carried around the outside of the wheel to *B*, so creating a flow of the fluid from *A* to *B* through the pump. Pumps of this kind are capable of producing a pressure difference of up to 200 kg wt per cm^2 and hence actuate a hydraulic ram so that it can push with a considerable force.

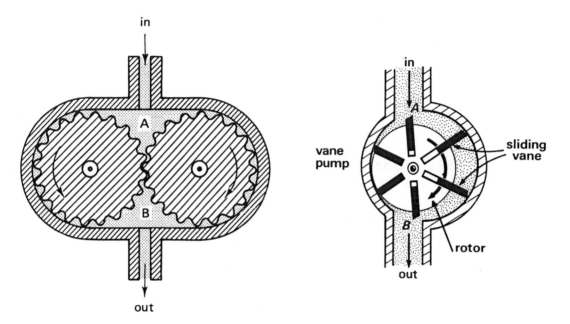

The vane pump has an off-centre rotor fitted with a number of sliding vanes which are sprung to press against the casing of the pump as the rotor turns. The vanes behave rather like the gear teeth in the gear pump, capturing a volume of fluid between themselves and the pump casing at *A* and carrying it around to *B*.

So far we have only considered hydraulics providing a linear motion, but hydraulic pumps can be used in reverse as hydraulic motors. So instead of driving the rotor of the vane pump, with an electric motor say, to provide a flow of hydraulic fluid, if the flow of fluid is produced by some other means, then the rotor will turn and provide a rotary output.

Hydraulics took off in the nineteenth century in a big way, largely due to the insight and drive of William Armstrong (1810–1900) who evolved hydraulic systems for quayside cranes, rotating winches, hydraulically opened lock gates, and a multitude of situations requiring large forces. London's Tower Bridge is opened hydraulically and one of the most interesting engineering structures of the twentieth century, the Thames Flood Barrier at Woolwich, depends on hydraulics for its operation. The great advantage of

153

hydraulically powered machines is that the power can be transmitted to them efficiently, quietly, and flexibly through pipes over considerable distances. Only the development of the electricity industry saw the demise of hydraulics in many situations, but the last 30 years has seen a resurgence of this very important technology, so that civil engineering equipment, aircraft, ships, agricultural machinery and robots rely very heavily on hydraulic rams and motors for their operation.

An interesting booklet which gives a brief history of the influence of hydraulics in the last century is *Hydraulic Machines* by Adrian Jarvis. Only 32 pages, but an eye-opener to the achievements of engineers in this field.

Exercise 11

1 The figure below shows four lever mechanisms. In each case the force P just balances the force Q. The measurements given are all centimetres. Decide (i) how far P moves relative to Q, and (ii) the relationship between P and Q, for each mechanism.

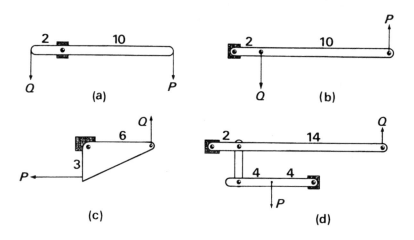

2 Piano keys are simple levers. Which class of lever are they, and how do they operate the hammers which strike the strings?

How does the mechanism differ between an upright piano and a grand piano?

How does the pedal mechanism of a piano operate?

3 Analyse the mechanism of a mechanical typewriter to see how the key operates the type bar.

4 Describe the operation of a claw hammer for extracting nails.

5 If a mother weighing 50 kg went on a seesaw with her daughter weighing 25 kg where would you expect them to sit?

6. The bow saw shown has its blade tensioned by pulling together the ends A and B of the saw frame. If the tension in the rod AB is T, what can you say about the tension in the saw blade?

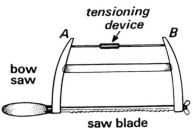

7 Explain the lever principle as it applies to
(a) a spanner;
(b) a wheelbarrow;
(c) a brace and bit drill;
(d) a cycle's brake lever;
(e) mobiles;
(f) the oar of a boat;
(g) a fishing rod;
(h) a person's arm;
(i) a spade.

8 Find the transmission factor of A relative to B in the mechanism below. If a force of 20 kg wt is applied downwards at A, what force is available at B?

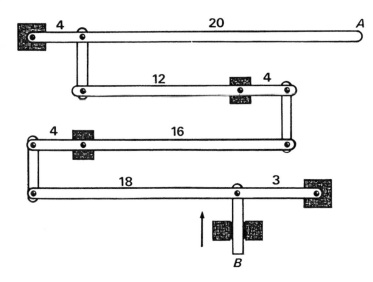

9 Archimedes is quoted as saying 'Give me a fulcrum on which to rest and I will move the Earth'. Explain this statement.

10 Two hydraulic rams *A*
    and *B* are connected by
    pressure tubing. *A* has a
    radius of 1 cm, *B* has a
    radius of 8 cm.

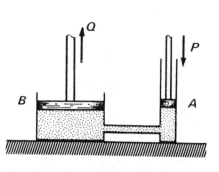

   (a) How far will *B* rise if
    A is pushed down
    16 cm?
   (b) If *A* is pushed down
    with a force of
    P = 6 kg wt, what
    force will the ram *B*
    be exerting?
   (c) If the pressure tubing is designed to withstand a
    maximum pressure of 20 kg wt per cm², what is the
    largest load which could be raised by ram *B*?

11 The ram in a master cylinder is actuated by pushing a
    lever as shown below. The master cylinder is connected
    by pressure tubing to 3 identical slave cylinders, and has
    a cross-sectional area of 15 cm², while the slave cylinders
    have a cross-sectional area of 10 cm².
   (a) How far do the pistons in the slave cylinders move
    compared to
     (i) the piston in the master cylinder?
     (ii) the handle of the lever?
   (b) How is the output force *Q* from each slave cylinder
    related to the input force *P* to the lever?

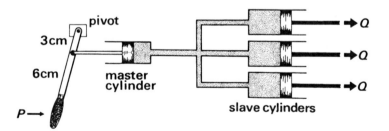

12 Four hydraulic rams *A, B, C* and *D* are linked together
    as in the following figure with the pistons of *B* and *C*
    physically linked to move together. The cross-sectional
    areas of the cylinders are 12 cm², 120 cm², 8 cm² and
    48 cm² respectively.

156

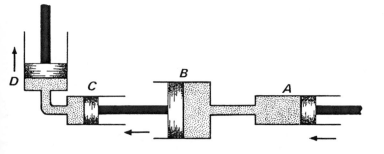

(a) How far does ram D move when ram A moves 20 cm?

(b) What load will ram D support when ram A is pushed with a force equivalent to 24 kg wt?

What will be the pressure in the hydraulic fluid (i) in A and B, (ii) in C and D, in this case?

13 Hydraulic fluid from a rotary pump enters the cylinder of a hydraulic ram at A and is drawn away at B (see below). The pump can pump the fluid at 18 cm³ s⁻¹ with a pressure difference of 150 kg wt cm⁻². Given that the area of cross-section of the cylinder is 6 cm² (i) what force can the ram exert and, (ii) at what speed will the ram be moving?

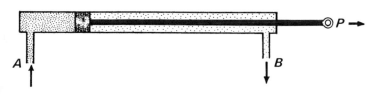

14 Design a mechanism for opening and shutting car windows.

15 A rotary vane actuator has a vane which is forced to rotate by pumping hydraulic fluid into one side of a cylindrical chamber and sucking it out from the other (see figure). The cylinder has an internal radius of 6 cm, and is 4 cm deep.

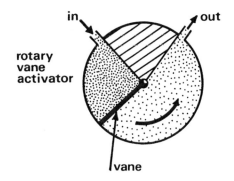

157

(a) What volume does the vane sweep out in turning through θ°?

(b) What must be the capacity of the pump in cm³ s⁻¹ if the vane is to turn at 5° per second?

(c) If the pump can produce a pressure difference of 20 kg wt per cm², what is the force turning the vane?

16 A new design of nutcrackers is made as shown.
   Find how far the handles of the nutcrackers move compared to the jaws of the nutcracker and hence compare the force Q with which the nut is cracked to the force P used to push the handles.

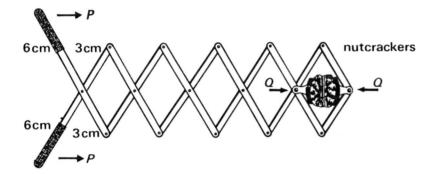

12 Mechanical manipulators

An analysis of robot designs

Automation, in the sense of using machines to carry out mechanical operations without human intervention, has been used by industry for over a hundred years. But robots which are computer controlled and capable of carrying out a multiplicity of tasks are a very recent phenomenon. They are often designed to have many degrees of movement, but in practice it is their reliability and their ability to repeat the same task over and over again with a high degree of accuracy, and without getting tired, or losing their concentration, which has led to them taking over many routine tasks on the shop floor. No matter how elaborate a robot, the basic movements involved are rotation and translation, and robots are classified by their joints. When an arm movement is achieved by a linear sliding motion or translation it is called a *prismatic joint*. When the arm movement is achieved by rotation it is called a *revolute joint*.

Depending on the configuration of joints in a robot, different sets of co-ordinates are required to describe its orientation and thus to program it, so robots often get named by the co-ordinate system which best fits their joints.

Cartesian robots

The figure below shows two examples of *cartesian* robots. The first operates rather like a gantry crane while the second is more like a tower crane. In each case the robot has 3 prismatic joints which allow a translation in 3 directions at right-angles to another. If the possible movements in the X, Y and Z directions are 4 m, 3 m and 2 m then the 'hand' of the robot can move to anywhere inside a cuboid with these dimensions. This accessible region is called the *working envelope* of the robot and is clearly an important design feature.

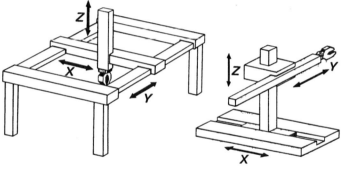

In moving the hand from one position to another the controlling computer will need to know the co-ordinates of the two points concerned. It can then carry out the movement required in a variety of ways. Much will depend on the sophistication of the robot and of the computer. The figure below shows 4 ways in which the robot might move the hand from A to B. The first of these is the least sophisticated and assumes the computer and robot can only move one of its

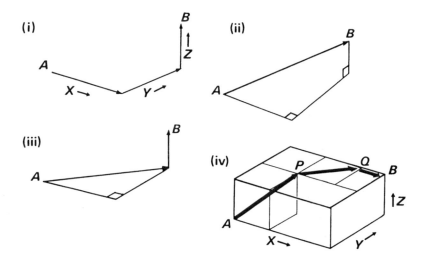

prismatic joints at a time, so it moves to B by carrying out its X translation, followed by its Y translation, and then its Z translation. The second solution shown takes the shortest, straight-line route from A to B, but this requires much more elaborate software and the ability of the robot to move its prismatic joints at three different speeds to correspond to the direction of AB. The third diagram shows a compromise between the first two solutions. Here the robot takes the shortest route in the XY plane until the hand is directly beneath B, and only then moves in the Z direction. The fourth route looks the most complicated, but could well happen in practice. It assumes that all the prismatic joints move at the same speed, so initially the hand moves along the diagonal of a cube to P, when it will have completed its Z movement. Then it moves along the diagonal of a square in the horizontal plane from P to Q when it will have completed its Y movement, and finally it moves from Q to B to complete the X movement required. All these solutions

have still not taken into account any objects which might get
in the way of the routes proposed and in a real situation, for
example spot welding part of a car, detours may be necessary.
But the beauty of a robot is that once the route has been
programmed the robot will carry it out repeatedly.

Cylindrical robots

Cylindrical robots have a
horizontal projecting radial
arm whose length can be
changed. The arm rotates
about a vertical axis through
one end and the arm can be
raised or lowered while
remaining horizontal. The
position of the hand can be
given by its distance r metres
from the vertical axis, the
angle θ through which it is
turned about the vertical axis
from a fixed direction, and its
height z metres above the
floor. In other words a typical
set of *cylindrical co-ordinates*.

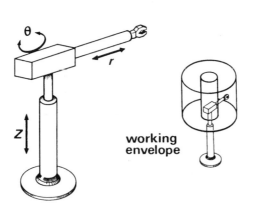

working envelope

  Because of its mode of operation its working envelope will
be the region between two cylinders as shown. The arm
cannot tilt up or down so it cannot reach down towards the
ground or up towards the ceiling.

  Suppose that it is necessary to move the hand of such a
robot from the position $(r, \theta, Z) = (0.8, 30, 1.3)$ to the
position $(1.5, 80, 1.5)$ as part of its function. Then it could
do this by extending its arm by 0.7 metres, turning about its
vertical axis through 50°, and climbing vertically through 0.2
metres, each one after the other in three distinct movements.
However, if the software and sophistication of the robot
were sufficient, it would carry out all three movements
simultaneously and take a spiral path between the points. In
practice it is likely that the robot will be programmed to take
the fastest route it is capable of. Why is it unlikely to be the
straight-line route between two points for this type of robot?

Spherical robot

The spherical robot has two revolute joints and one prismatic
joint. The arm can extend along its length, it can
rotate about a vertical axis, and thirdly it can be rotated

161

about a horizontal axis to elevate it above or below the horizontal. So the position of its hand can be described by the spherical co-ordinates (r, θ, φ) denoting the length of its arm, the direction in which it is pointing, and its angle of elevation.

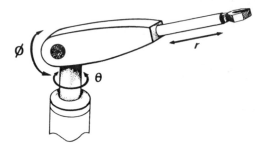

Compare it with fixing the position of a kite by giving the length of string, the bearing of the kite, and its angle of elevation from you as you fly it.

What will be the shape of the working envelope in this case?

Articulated robot

The articulated robot is not unlike the spherical robot, but instead of an extending arm it has an articulated arm rather like a human arm. This has the advantage that by bending at the elbow B the hand can be brought close to the shoulder A, which gives the robot a much larger working envelope than a spherical robot with the same length arm. The outer boundary of their working envelopes would be identical spherical surfaces but the articulated robot would be able to get its hand much nearer to A.

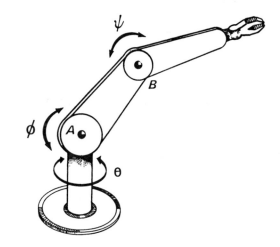

SCARA robot

The SCARA robot has a jointed arm like the articulated robot, but instead of moving in a vertical plane it rotates about vertical axes at A and B. This gives it a very flexible working envelope in the horizontal cross-section but its vertical movement is limited to the prismatic joint at C.

162

Suppose the range of values for θ is 270° and that the 'forearm' *BC* can be turned to within 30° of *AB*. If *AB* and *BC* are equal in length then the horizontal cross-section of the working envelope will look rather like a cardioid, but with a circle cut from its centre (see figure).

The arm *AB* is shown at one extreme position of its travel with arm *BC* pivoted as far around as it will go. The locus of *B* is confined to the arc of a circle centred at *A*, but the locus of *C* is all the region shown shaded.

This demonstrates rather nicely how one basic movement gives a one-dimensional locus but two basic movements allow the hand to move anywhere in a two-dimensional space. The position of *B* can be described by one co-ordinate θ, while the position of *C* is only known when both θ and φ are given.

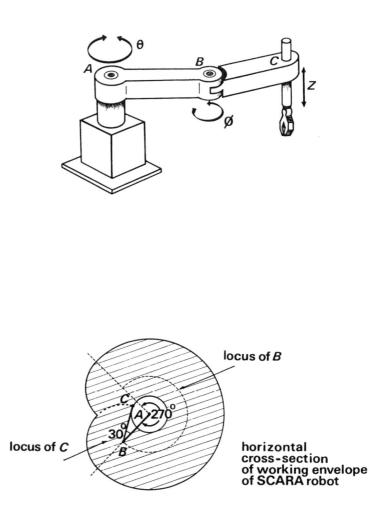

locus of *B*

locus of *C*

horizontal cross-section of working envelope of SCARA robot

There is nothing to stop robots being designed to have many-jointed arms, but there will always be some play in a joint, so the greater the number of joints the more inaccurate the robot is likely to be in achieving a particular position in space. With three basic movements, as in the five kinds of robots described, the robot will be able to position its hand in any point of its three-dimensional working envelope. To pin-point any particular point *three* co-ordinates will be needed and these will depend on the robot used. There is a very nice match between the various robots and the co-ordinate systems in general use by mathematicians, scientists and engineers to fix points in three dimensions, and the study of robot design helps towards the understanding of these systems.

163

End effectors

At the end of a robot arm is the 'hand', technically known as the *end effector*, and this can take a variety of forms depending on the use to which the robot is to be put. If it is being used to pick up and carefully place objects then it will need a means of gripping the object. This has resulted in many interesting designs for *grippers*. The figure below shows a selection of these.

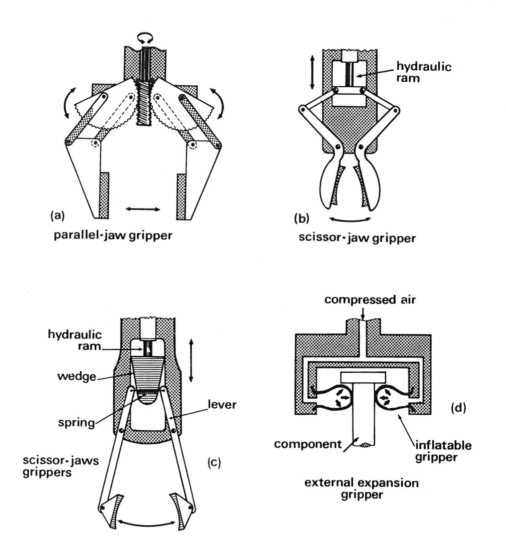

The *parallel-jaw grippers* make use of the parallelogram linkage so that the jaws remain parallel as they close on the object to be picked up. This makes the jaws suitable for picking up a wide range of objects with different widths.

In the example shown here the angle of each parallelogram linkage is changed by attaching one bar to a sprocket gear which is turned by a worm gear driven by an electric motor.

What affects the speed at which the jaws approach each other and the force they can exert?

The first *scissor-jaw grippers* (b) shown rely on a hydraulic (or pnematic) ram to actuate two variable-based triangle mechanisms to open and close the jaws, while the second example (c) uses a ram to drive a wedge between two levers to move the jaws together, and a spring to pull them apart. In a food packaging plant such a gripper would be used to pick up a bottle.

The fourth example shows the use of an *inflatable gripper* which is particularly useful when picking up fragile components such as glass containers.

Many other types of end effectors are used and the reader who is interested should refer to a specialist book such as *Elements of Industrial Robots* by Barry Leatham-Jones.

Assembly problems

Watching a young child trying fit objects into the holes of a posting box designed to improve manipulative skills will give some idea of the problems encountered in designing a robot to place bolts, for example, in closely fitting holes. Not only must the end of the bolt be placed precisely over the hole, but the bolt will need to be correctly aligned along the hole's axis. The human hand is very adept at making small adjustments to obtain the correct position, and some robots have been designed with special devices between the end of the arm and the gripper to enable similar adjustments to be made. These rely on our old friends the parallelogram linkage and the isosceles trapezium linkage.

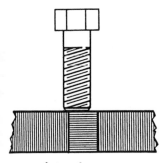

lateral error

(a)

angular error

(b)

The action of the parallelogram is by now well understood, but not so obvious is that by suitably arranging the ratios of the bars of the trapezium linkage the end of the component, in this case a bolt, stays put as BC and hence the bolt rotate. This property is explored in one of the exercises.

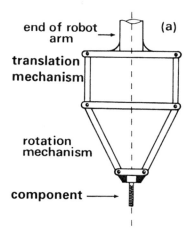

end of robot arm → (a)

translation mechanism

rotation mechanism

component →

mechanism for making small positional adjustments

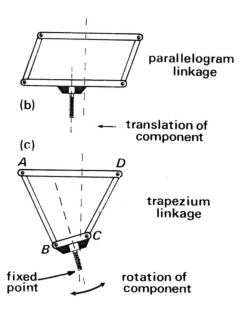

(b)

parallelogram linkage

← translation of component

(c)

A D

B C

trapezium linkage

fixed → point

rotation of component

Exercise 12

1   A cartesian robot is required to move the end of its arm 0.5 m in the X direction, 1.2 m in the Y direction and 0.3 m in the Z direction from point A to point B (see figure). The arm can be moved along the directions of its principal axes at 0.1 m/s.

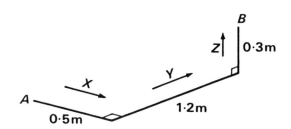

166

(a) If the robot is to move along one axis after the other
  (i) how long will it take to get from A to B?
  (ii) how many different alternative routes can the robot be programmed to take?

(b) If the robot can move along all three axes simultaneously, make a careful drawing to show the path taken by the end of the arm in travelling from A to B. How long will it take in this case?

(c) If the robot arm can be programmed to move at different speeds along its principal axes how could it be programmed to take the shortest route from A to B? How long will it take if 0.1 m/s is its maximum speed along an axis?

2 A cartesian robot is accurate to within ±0.02 mm in the X and Y directions and ±0.01 mm in the Z direction. How far out could it be (i) horizontally? (ii) overall?

3 A cylindrical robot can turn through $300°$ about its vertical axis. The end of its arm can extend from 0.5 m from the vertical axis to 1.0 m from the vertical axis, and it has a vertical travel of 0.4 m.

   Make a scale drawing of the horizontal cross-section of the robot's working envelope.

   What is the volume of the working envelope?

4 A cylindrical robot is to be programmed to move the end of its arm from the position $A(r, \theta, Z) =$ (0.5, 34, 0.8) to the position B (0.9, 124, 1.1) where r and Z are measured in metres and θ is measured in degrees. The robot can turn about its vertical axis at $15°/s$, extend its arm at 0.2 m/s and move vertically at 0.1 m/s.

(a) If the robot can only move one of its joints at a time:
  (i) find the time taken to move from A to B,
  (ii) make sketches to show the 6 alternative routes it can take.

(b) If all three motions start together and operate simultaneously:
  (i) sketch the path taken by the end of the arm,
  (ii) find the time to reach B.

(c) What is the length of the straight line path from A to B? Why is it unlikely the robot's arm would take this path?

*5 A cylindrical robot can extend its arm from 0.5 m to 1.3 m with an accuracy of 0.5 mm and turn through $270°$ with an accuracy of $0.1°$. Further, it can travel vertically through 0.3 m with an accuracy of 0.3 mm.

(a) Where in its envelope is the robot going to be
   (i) least accurate? (ii) most accurate?
(b) What is the greatest inaccuracy which can occur?

*6   A spherical robot can make complete revolutions about
   its vertical axis, turn its arm through ± 60° about its
   horizontal axis, and extend its arm from 0.6 m to 1 m.
   (a) Sketch the working envelope of the robot.
   (b) If it can rotate its arm about either revolute joint
       at 20°/s and extend its arm at 0.1 m/s, find the
       longest time it would take to travel between any
       two points in its working envelope if each joint acts
       (i) one after the other, (ii) together.

*7   An articulated robot can
   turn its arm AB about its
   shoulder A from the
   horizontal up to within
   10° of the vertical. The
   forearm BC can turn
   through 150° from the
   line of AB, i.e. from C to
   C' in the figure. It can
   make complete
   revolutions about its
   vertical axis.

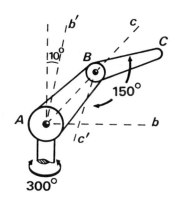

   Given that $AB = BC$ make careful drawings of the
   vertical and horizontal cross-sections of the working
   envelope through A.

*8   A SCARA robot can turn
   its arm AB through 240°
   about a vertical axis
   through A. The arm BC
   can turn 45° clockwise
   and 150° anticlockwise
   from the line AB about a
   vertical axis through B.
   Make a scale drawing of
   the horizontal cross-
   section of the working
   envelope of the robot
   given that $AB = 1.2$ m
   and $BC = 0.8$ m.

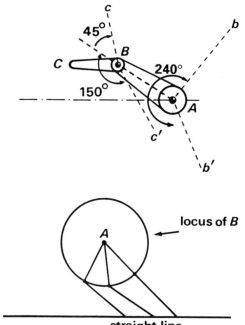

*9   It is not easy for a robot
   with an articulated arm to
   follow a straight line
   path. To investigate this
   draw a circle of radius

3 cm to represent the locus of the 'elbow' B and, assuming the forearm BC is also 3 cm, look at the positions of the robot arm as it traces out a line whose nearest point to A is 4.5 cm.

10 Use a construction kit to make models of (i) a parallel-jaw gripper and (ii) a scissor-jaw gripper.

11 A scissor-jaw gripper consists of two levers actuated by a wedge. The pivot points are 8 cm from the wedge and 4 cm from the centre of the jaw. If the angle of the wedge is 20°, what is the ratio of the distance moved by the jaws to the distance moved by the wedge?

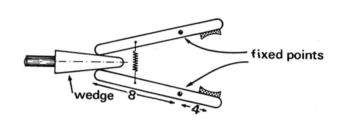

12 Make a trapezium linkage $ABCD$ and attach a long isosceles triangle to the side BC as shown. Make a line of small holes down the line of symmetry of the triangle and investigate their loci as AD is held and BC is rocked. Try to find a mechanism of this type which leaves a point P of the triangle virtually at rest as BC rocks. Such a mechanism is used to give rotational adjustments to an end effector.

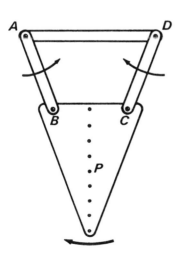

Solutions

Exercise 1

1   (a) $+5$, (b) -2, (c) $+\frac{1}{6}$, (d) $-\frac{2}{3}$, (e) -8, (f) -20, (g) $+\frac{1}{64}$.

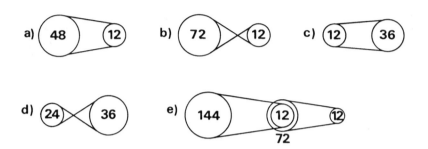

2   Other possible transmission factors include:
$$+2, \ +3, \ +8, \ +\tfrac{3}{4}, \ +12, \ +36$$
and their negation or reciprocal, or any product or quotient.

Transmission factors which are not possible include $+5$, $+7$, $+11$.

Possible integral transmission factors from $+1$ to $+36$ are:

1, 2, 3, 4, 6, 8, 9, 12, 16, 18, 24, 27, 32, 36,

that is all integers expressible in the form $2^p \ 3^q$.
It follows that the same results could be achieved using only pulleys with diameter 12 mm, 24 mm, and 36 mm.

3   Fan speed $= \dfrac{10}{7.5} \times 3000 = 4000$ rpm

Alternator speed $= \dfrac{10}{5} \times 3000 = 6000$ rpm

4   420 stitches per minute. 1680 rpm.

5   $\dfrac{2}{36} \times 3000 \simeq 167$ rpm.

6   $t(AB) = \frac{1}{2}$ $t(AC) = \frac{1}{2} \times \frac{13}{30} \times \frac{13}{30} = \frac{169}{1800} \simeq \frac{1}{11}$

Engine speed $= \dfrac{100}{20\pi} \times 60 \times \dfrac{1800}{169} \simeq 1017$ rpm

7   720 rpm. 3.6π m/s.

8   $\frac{150}{10} = 15$ and $\frac{150}{25} = 6$. $\frac{192}{8} \times 2 = 48$ rps.

9

	14	17	20	35	28
32	2.29	1.88	1.60	1.33	1.14
50	3.57	2.94	2.50	2.08	1.79

10 Chain wheel 140 teeth, free wheel 14 teeth. If the chain wheel were much larger it would touch the ground, and if the free wheel had fewer teeth the chain would jump over the teeth.

11 BMX: 40 inch gear.

For a 27 inch wheel to have the same gear the transmission factor between chain wheel and free wheel would be $\frac{40}{27} \simeq 1.48$. A chain wheel with 28 teeth driving a free wheel with 19 teeth leads to a gear of 39.8 inches which is a good approximation.

12

		16	20	24	28	32	36	free wheel
	32	52	41.6	34.7	29.7	26	23.1	
chain	40	65	52	43.3	37.1	32.5	28.9	gear in
wheel	48	78	62.4	52	44.6	39	34.7	inches

Gear	Chain wheel	Free wheel	Gear	Chain wheel	Free wheel
23.1	32	36	41.6	32	20
26	32	32	43.3	40	24
28.9	40	36	44.6	48	28
29.7	32	28	52	32	16
32.5	40	32		40	20
34.7	32	24		48	24
	48	36	62.4	48	20
37.1	40	28	65	40	16
39	48	32	78	48	16

An analysis like this shows up the shortcomings of such a gear arrangement. Not all the combinations give different gears, while some are very close e.g. 28.9 to 29.7, and others have large gaps e.g. 65 to 78. In practice it is highly unlikely that a cyclist would go through all the gears in order, because of the need to move the chain between both sets of sprockets at almost every change in the sequence.

13 The hub ratio gives the number of revolutions of the rear wheel for each revolution of the free wheel.

First: 52 inch   second: 67 inch   third: 78 inch
fourth: 88 inch.

14   $4 < d < 20$. 4 cm lateral movement. $\frac{1}{5} < t < 5$.

15   (a) 67.4 cm (b) $2\sqrt{288} + 4.92 + 19.11) \simeq 82.0$ cm
     (c) $\sqrt{143} + \sqrt{143} + \sqrt{140} + 9.38 + 6.28 + 3.69 \simeq$
     55.1 cm

17   They are less likely to slip.
21   So that the belt only has one surface and wears evenly.
22   The belt lengths between pulleys must remain parallel
     to each other, so the diameter of A must equal the total
     of the diameters of B, C and D.

Exercise 2

1   (a) -4, (b) $+\frac{1}{5}$, (c) $+9$, (d) -48, (e) $+\frac{1}{20}$, (f) $+\frac{1}{15}$.

2

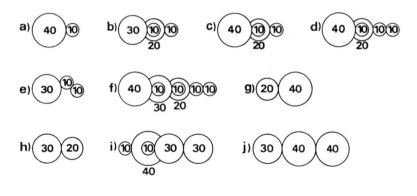

3   1st gear $= t(AD) \times t(FC) = \quad -\frac{24}{48} \times -\frac{16}{56} = +\frac{1}{7}$

    2nd gear $= t(AD) \times t(EB) = \quad -\frac{24}{48} \times -\frac{32}{40} = +\frac{2}{5}$

top gear $=$ direct drive $= +1$

reverse $= t(AD) \times t(GH) \times t(HC)$

    $= -\frac{24}{48} \times -\frac{12}{12} \times -\frac{12}{56} = -\frac{3}{28}$

    When $t(AD) = -\frac{27}{45} = -\frac{3}{5}$ then:

    1st gear $= +\frac{6}{35}$, 2nd gear $= +\frac{12}{25}$, top gear $= +1$,

$$\text{reverse} = -\frac{9}{70}$$

If A, D, F, C, G and H are as before, but B has 18 teeth and E has 54 teeth, then the highest gear will be obtained when B meshes with E giving

$$t(AB) = t(AD) \times t(EB) = \quad -\frac{24}{48} \times -\frac{54}{18} = +\frac{3}{2}.$$

4 1st gear $= t(AB) \times t(ER) = \quad -\frac{1}{3} \times -\frac{16}{32} = +\frac{1}{6}.$ 667 rpm.

2nd gear $= t(AB) \times t(DQ) = -\frac{1}{3} \times -\frac{20}{28} = +\frac{5}{21}.$ 952 rpm.

3rd gear $= t(AB) \times t(CP) = \quad -\frac{1}{3} \times -\frac{28}{20} = +\frac{7}{15}.$ 1867 rpm.

top gear $= t(AP) = +1,$ 4000 rpm

5 (i) Bottom roller $= t(AB) \times t(CD)$

$$= -\frac{12}{32} \times -\frac{12}{32} = +\frac{9}{64}.$$

(ii) Top roller $= -\frac{9}{64}.$

6 46 rpm

7 25 cutting blades every revolution.   2.39 cm.

8 $315 = 3 \times 3 \times 5 \times 7$ (see figure)

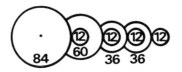

9 Transmission factor $= \frac{1}{50} \times \frac{1}{2} \times \frac{1}{3} = \frac{1}{300}.$

Follower's speed $=$ 10 rpm.

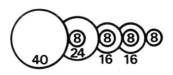

10 (a) $60 \ = 5 \times 3 \times 2 \times 2$ (see figure)

(b) $240 = 40 \times 3 \times 2$ (see figure)

16 (a) 4500 rpm   (b) 2000 rpm

17 (a) $\dfrac{\omega_A + \omega}{\omega_S - \omega} = \dfrac{t_S}{t_R} = \dfrac{1}{3}$

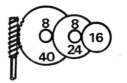

(i) $\omega_S = 600$ and $\omega = 0$, so $\omega_A = 200$ rpm.

(ii) $\omega = 600$ and $\omega_S = 0$, so $\omega_A = -800$ rpm.

(b) $\dfrac{\omega_P + \omega}{\omega_S - \omega} = \dfrac{t_S}{t_P} = 1$,

so given $\omega_P = 0$ and $\omega_S = 600$, then $\omega = 300$ rpm.

(c) $\omega = 600$ and $\omega_A = 200$, so $\omega_S = 3000$ rpm.

18 $\dfrac{\omega_C + \omega}{\omega_A - \omega} = \dfrac{t_A}{t_C}$, so when $\omega_C = 0$ and $\omega_A = 12\omega$, then

$$\frac{\omega}{12\omega - \omega} = \frac{12}{t_C} \Rightarrow t_C = 132$$

Now $t_A + 2t_B = t_C \Rightarrow t_B = 60$

19 Given $t_B = kt_A$, then $t_C = t_A + 2t_B = (1 + 2k)t_A$

Hence $\dfrac{\omega_C + \omega}{\omega_A - \omega} = \dfrac{t_A}{t_C} = \dfrac{1}{1 + 2k}$.

(a) $\omega = 0$ giving $\omega_A = (1 + 2k)\omega_C$.

(b) $\omega_C = 0$ giving $(1 + 2k)\omega = \omega_A - \omega \Rightarrow \omega_A = (2 + 2k)\omega$.

(c) $\omega_A = 0$ giving $(1 + 2k)(\omega_C + \omega) = -\omega$

$\Rightarrow \omega_C = -(2 + 2k)\omega/(1 + 2k)$.

20

		$k = 1$	$k = 2$	$k = \frac{1}{2}$
$t(AC) = \dfrac{\omega_C}{\omega_A} = \dfrac{1}{1 + 2k}$		$\dfrac{1}{3}$	$\dfrac{1}{5}$	$\dfrac{1}{2}$
$t(AR) = \dfrac{\omega}{\omega_A} = \dfrac{1}{2 + 2k}$		$\dfrac{1}{4}$	$\dfrac{1}{6}$	$\dfrac{1}{3}$
$t(RC) = \dfrac{\omega_C}{\omega} = -\left(\dfrac{2 + 2k}{1 + 2k}\right)$		$-\dfrac{4}{3}$	$-\dfrac{6}{5}$	$-\dfrac{3}{2}$

$t(CA)$, $t(RA)$ and $t(CR)$ are then the reciprocals of the above.

Now $t(RC) = -\left(\dfrac{2 + 2k}{1 + 2k}\right) = -\left(1 + \dfrac{1}{1 + 2k}\right)$

and as $0 < k < \infty$ it follows that

$$-2 < t(RC) < -1$$

Exercise 3

1 As an example suppose $AC = 6$ cm and $BC = 4$ cm, then

x (cm)	2	2.5	3	4	5	6	7	8	9	10
θ (degrees)	0	29	36	41	41	39	35	29	21	0

From the graph
(i) min $\theta = 0°$
(ii) max $\theta = 42°$
The maximum value of θ
will occur when BC is
perpendicular to AB
giving $\sin \theta = \frac{4}{6}$ which
confirms max $\theta = 42°$ to
the nearest degree.
   θ does not change in
equal amounts for equal
changes in x.

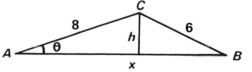

2

x (cm)	3	4	5	6	7	8	9	10
θ (degrees)	40	47	49	48	47	44	41	37
h (cm)		5.1	5.8	6.0	6.0	5.8	5.6	5.2	4.8

The answers can be achieved by (i) using a model, (ii)
scale drawing, or (iii) using trigonometry.

From the diagram the cosine rule gives

$$6^2 = 8^2 + x^2 - 16x \cos \theta$$

175

Hence

$$\cos \theta = \frac{28 + x^2}{16x}$$

to enable θ to be calculated for different values of x.
Then $h = 8 \sin \theta$

3 Using a model or trigonometry

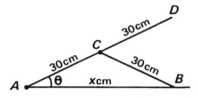

$$x = 60 \cos \theta$$

$\theta°$	15	30	45	60
x cm	58	52	42.4	30

Hinge a strut of length 30 cm to C, the middle of the desk top, and make notches for B at the distances from A given in the table.

4 If AC is of length d and $\angle CAB = \theta$
then

$$x = 2d \cos \theta$$
$$\text{and} \quad y = 2d \sin \theta$$
$$\text{so} \quad x^2 + y^2 = 4d^2,$$

the equation of a circle.

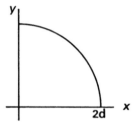

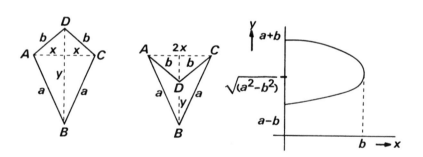

5 Let $AD = DC = b$, $AB = BC = a$, where $a > b$, and let $AC = 2x$,
then

$$y = BD = \sqrt{(a^2 - x^2)} \pm \sqrt{(b^2 - x^2)}$$

6 The locus of C is a circle as it is a fixed distance from the fixed point A. Normally P will trace out an ellipse, but when $PC = AC = CB$ then P traces out a straight line through A and perpendicular to AB.

7   Let the legs be pivoted about their middle then, by Pythagoras' theorem

$$x^2 + y^2 = 50^2$$

so

$$x = \sqrt{(2500-y^2)}$$

where y is half the required height and x is half the distance AB.

h (cm)	60	65	70	75	80
y	30	32.5	35	37.5	40
x	40	38	35.7	33	30
AB	80	76	71.4	66	60

Have one set of legs hinged to the board at A and have notches for B so that AB has the above lengths.

8   $60° \leqslant$ angle $ACB \leqslant 113°$
2 m below the height of C to 1.56 m above the height of C, a variation of 3.56 m.
DC horizontal when $AB = 1.5\sqrt{2} \simeq 2.12$ m
Maximum speed when DC horizontal, so D then 4 m from axis BC and travelling on a circle with circumference 8π m.
So maximum angular speed is $(11 \times 60)/8\pi \simeq 26$ rpm

9   Let the struts of the framework be 80 cm long, then by Pythagoras' theorem

$$AB^2 = 80^2 - h^2,$$

so
$h = 28$ gives $AB = 74.9$ cm, and
$h = 36$ gives $AB = 71.4$ cm.

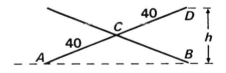

10   θ changes from 46.0° to 129.8°, i.e. through 83.2°.
The extreme positions of W are 31.9 cm apart.

11   When $AB = 2$ m, triangle ABC is equilateral, and as the jib is to be horizontal, it follows that BC is at 60° to the horizontal. To raise the jib to 80° the angle $BCA = 140°$ which makes $AB \simeq 3.76$ m.

177

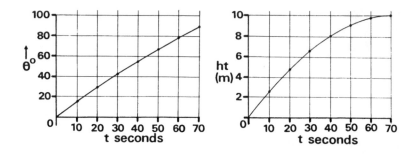

12 When CA is horizontal $AB = 10\sqrt{2}$ m so it takes $50\sqrt{2}$
    $\simeq 71$ seconds to raise the derrick to the vertical.
       After t seconds from the $\theta = 0$ position $AB =$
    $(10\sqrt{2} - t/5)$ m so taking $t = 0,10,\ldots, 70$ it is possible
    to calculate the corresponding values for angle BCA and
    hence θ, and the height of A.

t seconds	0	10	20	30	40	50	60	70
nearest degree	0	15	29	42	54	66	78	89
height of A (metres)	0	2.6	4.8	6.7	8.1	9.1	9.8	10

13 A moves on the arc of a circle centre C.
    When flat, D is approximately $75 + 70 + 44 = 189$ cm
    from B.

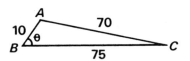

$$\cos \theta = \frac{10^2 + 75^2 - 70^2}{2 \times 10 \times 75} \Rightarrow \theta \simeq 57°$$

hence ladder at $33°$ to vertical.
    B approximately $3.2 \cos 33° = 2.7$ m above the floor.
Maximum height reached by D is 1 metre.

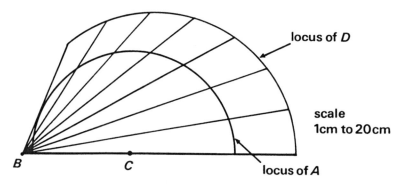

locus of D

scale
1cm to 20cm

locus of A

14 X and Y will be 1 m and 2 m high respectively.
    To be quite safe the driver should stop 1 m from the
    door, although in practice X will not move outwards
    1 m until it is above the height of the car. Y moves on
    a straight line parallel to, and 2 m from, the ground.

178

16   The throw of the piston is twice the length of AC and independent of the length of BC.

17   The throw of the needle is twice the length of AC, and is independent of the length of BC. However $BC > AC$ for the mechanism to operate.

   To give a swing needle movement the guide would need to be pivoted and oscillated by a cam, or by another variable-based triangle mechanism.

18   R_1 ranges from 0.9 m to 1.4 m
   R_2 ranges from 1.0 m to 1.75 m
   R_3 ranges from 0.8 m to 1.3 m.

19   (a) $\dfrac{BC}{AC} = \cos 30° \simeq 0.866$

   Possible dimensions: $AC = 15$ m, $BC = 13$ cm

   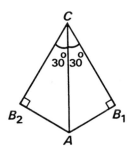

   (b) $\cos^{-1} \frac{14}{20} \simeq 45.6° \Rightarrow$ angle $B_2CB_1 \simeq 91°$

      so the ratio feed time : return time $\simeq 3:1$
   (c)   For a ratio of 8:1, angle $B_2CB_1 = 40° \Rightarrow BC = 20\cos 20°$
      $\Rightarrow BC = 18.3$ cm to 3 sig. figs.
   (d)   If $BC > AC$, AD will not oscillate, but will make complete revolutions about A. Investigate how the speed of rotation varies.

20   Best understood by making a model.
   A good exercise in scale drawing. Use 30° intervals for the angle turned through by BC.
   Results can be calculated but this is tedious unless a computer is used.

21   Let $AB = 2y$ and $NC = x$
   then
      $x^2 + y^2 = 100$
   so
      $AB = 2\sqrt{(100 - x^2)}$

   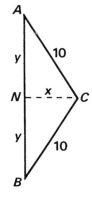

   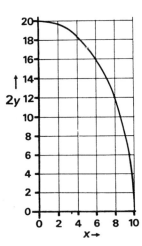

179

Exercise 4

6 P,Q,R and T move on the arcs of circles, radius AD, with centres on the line DC. S moves on the arc of a circle centred at C with radius CS.

   When AD is at $60°$ to DC, all the points on AB will be moving in a direction perpendicular to AD, that is, at $30°$ to DC.

7 (a) DC moves in the opposite direction to AF, and twice as far as AF. That is, a factor of -2.
   (b) Three times as far in the same direction. Scale factor $+3$.
      (i) $+1 <$ scale factor $< +3$ (ii) scale factor $+3$
   (c) None.

8 (a) 3 times as far to the left. Scale factor -3
   (b) $\frac{1}{2}$ as far down. Scale factor $-\frac{1}{2}$.
   (c) G, B, D and F trace out arcs of circles.
      The other point of the linkage which traces out a straight line is the point of EF intersected by the line AC produced.

9 (a) (i) $+3$ (ii) $+4$
   (b) (i)   fix X, object at T, image at Y
      (ii)   fix X, object at T, image at Z
      (iii) fix Y, object at Z, image at T
      (iv) fix Y, object at T, image at Z
      (v)   fix Y, object at X, image at Z
      (vi) fix Y, object at T, image at X

10 3 linkages capable of enlarging with a l.s.f. of 4 are shown above, in each of which O is fixed, P traces the object and Q traces the image. But other linkages are possible.

11 A half turn about A followed by a half turn about B is equivalent to a translation through $2AB$.

12 The frog can jump $6(4\cos 15° - 4\cos 75°) \simeq 17$ cm.

180

3 (a) *DT* stays horizontal, but all points on it move on circular arcs, of radius *BC*, with centres on *AB*.
   (b) Arc of a circle, centre *C*, radius *CT*.
   (c) Arc of a circle, centre *B*, radius *BT*.

14 The smallest change in the angle occurs when the movement is symmetric.

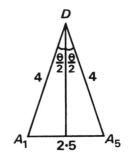

$$\sin\frac{\theta}{2} = \frac{1.25}{4}$$

$$\Rightarrow \theta \simeq 36.4°$$

15 (a) $\pi(54^2 - 18^2) \times \dfrac{140}{360} = 3167$ cm

   (b) (i) As *ABCD* is a parallelogram with $AB = DC = 48$ cm, all points of *BC* and anything attached rigidly to it will move on arcs of circles with radius 48 cm.

       (ii) The shaded region *XYZT* can be imagined as made up of many thin vertical strips of length 40 cm which can be sheared into a rectangle of dimensions *XT* and *XY*. Now *XT* is equal to the sideways movement of the blade *PQ* which is 48 sin 60° each side off its symmetric position, so $XY = 96 \sin 60°$.

   (c) The area changes, for if the wiper goes from α to the vertical to $(120° - \alpha)$ to the vertical then the area swept out will be equivalent to a rectangle of 40 cm by $48(\sin \alpha + \sin (120° - \alpha))$ cm.

16 (a) The angle of *DA* is fixed.
       ABCD is a parallelogram, so *CB* parallel to *DA*.
       CEFG is a parallelogram, so *GF* parallel to *CE*, and hence to *DA*.
   (b) (i) Higher and closer to the wall bracket.
       (ii) No change.
   (c) Rotate *CG*.

18 (a) *R*: 1 cm, *S*: 3 cm, *T*: 5 cm, *U*: 7 cm, *V*: 9 cm, *C*: 10 cm.
   (b) Parts of ellipses with major axes 3, 5, 7 and 9 times as long as their minor axes.
   (c) If *x* and *y* are the lengths of the diagonals of the basic rhombus of the mechanism when the links are at an angle of θ to the vertical, then
       $$x = y \tan \theta$$

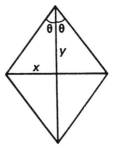

Now $AC = 5x = 5y \tan \theta$ and $XY \simeq y$, so
$AC \simeq 5XY \tan \theta$.

(d) As X and Y are squeezed together θ increases, and as $\tan \theta$ increases with θ it follows that $AC : XY$ increases.

Exercise 5

1   The motion of AB relative to DC is the motion of DC relative to AB.

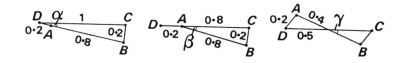

(i) $\alpha \simeq 11.5°$ (ii) $\beta \simeq 14.4°$ (iii) $\gamma \simeq 22.3°$

8   (a) Let N be the mid-point of PQ, then $AN \perp PQ$.
Now $OP \times OQ = (PN + NO)(QN - NO)$
$\qquad\qquad\qquad = (PN + NO)(PN - NO)$
$\qquad\qquad$ as $PN = QN$
$\qquad\qquad\qquad = PN^2 - NO^2$
$\qquad\qquad\qquad = a^2 - h^2 - (b^2 - h^2)$
$\qquad\qquad\qquad = a^2 - b^2$

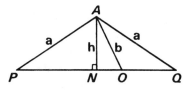

(b) (i) a straight line (ii) a circle
(c) Q traces out part of a circle unless P moves along a straight line through O, when Q will also move on along the same straight line.

Exercise 6

4   A possible solution is shown in the figure.

15   (a) $\cos \alpha_1 = \dfrac{7^2 + 4^2 - 8^2}{2 \times 4 \times 7} \Rightarrow \alpha_1 \simeq 89°$

$\cos \alpha_2 = \dfrac{7^2 + 4^2 - 4^2}{2 \times 4 \times 7} \Rightarrow \alpha_2 \simeq 29°$

So AD can oscillate through $60°$

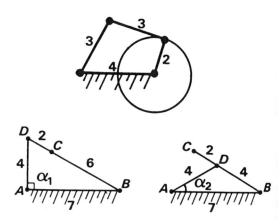

(b) $\cos\beta_1 = \dfrac{7^2 + 6^2 - 6^2}{2 \times 7 \times 6} \Rightarrow \beta_1 \simeq 54.3°$

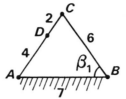 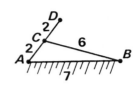

$\cos\beta_2 = \dfrac{7^2 + 6^2 - 2^2}{2 \times 7 \times 6} \Rightarrow \beta_2 \simeq 15.4°$

So *BC* can oscillate through 39°

(c) The shorter rocker arm oscillates through the larger angle.

16 To rock through 90° the rockers will need to be at 45° to *AB* in their extreme positions. By taking a suitable value for *x*, the value of $(x + y)$ and hence *y* can easily be determined using the cosine rule. For example $x=4$ and $y=13.4$ gives angle *DAB* as 44.95° and a very good approximation for internal rocking angles of 90°. If whole number solutions are preferred, then $x = 7$ and $y = 9$ gives angle *DAB* as 46.4.

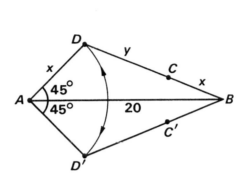

17 *AD* will be at one extremity when *DC* passes through *B* as in fig. 25. To obtain a rocking angle of 120° angle *DAB* will also have to be 120°. The length of *AD* can now be chosen and the length *DB* calculated using the cosine rule. Taking *AD* as 6 cm gives a particularly neat result, for then $DB=14$ cm and hence, due to symmetry, $BC=6$ cm, giving $DC=20$ cm.

Solving problems where the external rocking angles are different needs careful analysis and a model is a great help to focus one's thinking. But all that is needed is good spatial insight and application of the cosine rule.

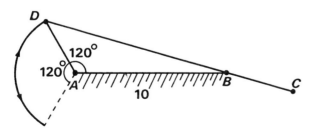

18 Concentrate on a pair of opposite angles of the quadrilateral linkage. It is always possible to manipulate the linkage to a position so that the two angles add up to more than 180°, and then to a position where their angle sum is less than 180°, so by a continuity argument there is a position in between where the angle sum is 180°, the condition for a cyclic quadrilateral.

19 When it is cyclic. The area of a quadrilateral is given by the formula

$$[(s - a)(s - b)(s - c)(s - d) - abcd \cos^2 (B + D)/2]^{\frac{1}{2}}$$

where s is half the perimeter, so it is a maximum when $\cos(B + D)/2 = 0$, that is when $B + D = 180°$, the condition for a cyclic quadrilateral. Proof of this formula may be found in *Advanced Trigonometry* by Durell and Robson.

20 (i) Yes, when one angle is a reflex angle. As the reflex angle increases in size the other three angles decrease.
   (ii) Yes, any convex quadrilateral when manipulated will increase the sizes of one pair of opposite angles.
   (iii) Yes, when one angle is reflex. As the reflex angle is reduced in size the other three angles increase.
   (iv) No, as the angle sum is constant.

21 There is no obvious result for the angle sum of the cross-over linkage as
$$\angle A + \angle B + \theta = 180°$$
and
$$\angle D + \angle C + \theta = 180°$$
giving
$$\angle A + \angle B + \angle C + \angle D = 360° - 2\theta,$$
but θ varies with the position of the linkage. However,
$$\angle A + \angle B = 180° - \theta = \angle C + \angle D.$$

Exercise 7

1 18π cm/s. 4 times as fast.

2 $t(AW) = t(AB) \times t(CD) = \frac{1}{3} \times \frac{1}{4} = \frac{1}{12}$, and as the radius of the crank is $\frac{1}{4}$ of the radius of the winding drum, $t(PQ) = \frac{1}{48}$.

184

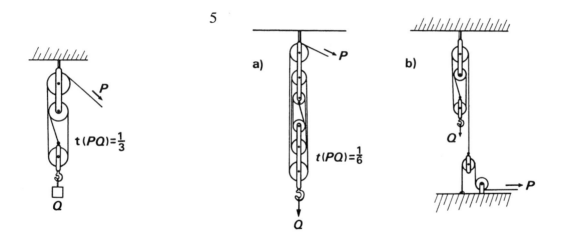

4 If D moves up d metres the rope from C to B will need to be pulled down $2d$ metres. To do this the rope under A will need to be pulled $4d$ metres.
Hence $t(PQ) = \frac{1}{4}$.
P will need to be pulled 48 metres.

6 $t(QP) = \frac{1}{8}$. Another pulley would make $t(QP) = \frac{1}{16}$.
N such pulleys would have a transmission factor of 2^{1-N}.

7 Many solutions, for example:
(a) two blocks each with 6 pulleys.
(b) one system like that in question 6 using 3 pulleys to give a factor of 4, combined with a system like that in question 3 to give a factor of 3.

8 $t(PQ) = t(AB) \times t(CD) \times \dfrac{\text{radius } E}{\text{radius } P} = \dfrac{1}{3} \times \dfrac{1}{5} \times \dfrac{1}{5} = \dfrac{1}{75}$

9 Transmission factor $= \dfrac{10 - 9.5}{2 \times 10} = \dfrac{1}{40}$.

Weight lifted $= 20 \times 40 \times 50\% = 400$ kg wt.

10    $\dfrac{a-12}{2a} = \dfrac{1}{50} \Rightarrow \alpha = 12.5.$

12   (a)   Revolutions in 30 minutes = $30 \times 60 = 1800$

       (i)   Thickness of tape = $1.5 \div 1800 = 1/1200$ cm

       (ii)   Length of tape = $\dfrac{\text{cross sectional area of tape}}{\text{thickness of tape}}$

$$= \pi \,(2.5^2 - 1^2) \times 1200 \text{ cm}$$
$$= 198 \text{ metres approx.}$$

   (b) $\frac{2}{5} < t(TS) < \frac{5}{2}$

   (c)   After t seconds the driving wheel T will have t thicknesses of tape on it, so its effective radius will then be

$$(1 + t/1200) \text{ cm.}$$

The amount of tape wound on reel T will be proportional to the cross-sectional area of tape, namely

$$\pi \,[(1 + t/1200)^2 - 1] \text{ cm}^2,$$

so the tape left on reel S will correspondingly be proportional to its cross-sectional area, namely

$$\pi \,(2.5^2 - 1) - \pi \,[(1 + t/1200)^2 - 1]$$
$$= \pi \,[2.5^2 - (1 + t/1200)^2].$$

If the radius of S at this time is r, then

$$\pi \,(r^2 - 1) = \pi \,[2.5^2 - (1 + t/1200)^2]$$

giving

$$r = [7.25 - (1 + t/1200)^2]^{\frac{1}{2}}$$

The transmission factor after t seconds is the ratio of these radii which can be written as

$$\left[\frac{7.25}{(1 + t/1200)^2} - 1 \right]^{-\frac{1}{2}}$$

   (d)   The tape will be travelling at 11 cm/s when the circumference of T is 11 cm. This will be when its radius is $11 \div 2\pi = 1.75$ cm, and happens when

$$1 + t/1200 = 1.75$$
$$\Rightarrow t = 900 \text{ s} = 15 \text{ min.}$$

3 (a) 942 metres
(b) The effective radius of each drum will be different, except when both cages are halfway, so one revolution of the drums will mean a different displacement of the cages.
(c) Let a be the length wound onto drum A in n revolutions, then

$$a = \pi 2 + \pi (2 + 0.02) + \pi (2 + 2 \times 0.02)$$
$$+ \ldots + \pi (2 + (n-1) \times 0.02)$$
$$\Rightarrow a = n \pi [2 + 0.01 (n-1)] \text{ sum of an}$$
arithmetic progression (A.P.)

Let b be the length unwound from drum B in n revolutions, then

$$b = \pi 4 + \pi(4 - 0.02) + \pi(4 - 2 \times 0.02) + \ldots +$$
$$\pi(4 - (n-1) \times 0.02)$$

$$\Rightarrow b = n \pi [4 - 0.01 (n-1)] \text{ sum of an A.P.}$$

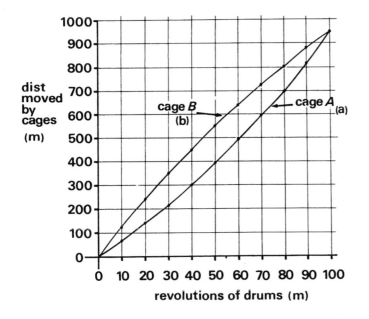

14 One solution is to use winding drums of different diameters on the same shaft. A second solution is to have winding drums of the same diameter on different shafts linked by

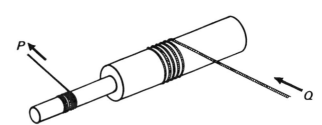

gears, or pulleys and belts. Another solution is to use a pulley system. One based on paper clips like that described in the text works very effectively, but strictly limits the length of string which can be pulled out.

15

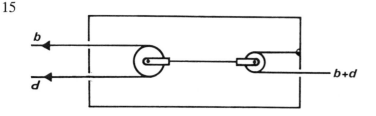

16 r moves 5 cm. Subtraction: $p-q$.

17 (i) 12 lengths. 12 metres. 10 tonnes weight.
    (ii) 14 tonnes weight
    (iii) 2 m/s.

Exercise 8

1 The centre does not stay parallel to the ground as the triangle rolls. The centre does not stay in the same place as the drill rotates.

3 As the triangles used in the construction are equilateral, all the arcs subtend $\frac{\pi}{3}$ radians at their respective centres. In the first curve the boundary with 3 arcs has length $3 \times 5 \times \frac{\pi}{3} = 5\pi$ cm.

In the second curve there are 3 arcs with radius 4 cm and 3 arcs with radius 1 cm, so the total length of the boundary is $3 \times 4 \times \frac{\pi}{3} + 3 \times 1 \times \frac{\pi}{3} = 5\pi$ cm.

In this particular question the arcs can easily be seen to be $\frac{1}{6}$ of a circle so the formula $s=r\theta$ is not really needed. However, it is useful when finding the perimeters of asymmetric shapes.

4 2 lines lead to a circle.

5 Let XY be rotated about A through an angle α radians to trace out arcs a_1 and a_2, and let $AX = x$ and let $AX = x$ and $AY = y$,
    then
    $$a_1 = \alpha x \text{ and } a_2 = \alpha y$$

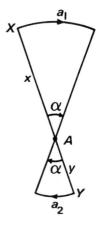

so
$$a_1 + a_2 = \alpha (x + y) = \alpha XY.$$

Similarly by rotating the diameter in turn
about B through angle β from l_2 to l_3
about C through angle γ from l_3 to l_4
about D through angle δ from l_4 to l_1

$$b_1 + b_2 = \beta XY, \quad c_1 + c_2 = \gamma XY, \quad d_1 + d_2 = \delta XY$$

so the perimeter is $(\alpha + \beta + \gamma + \delta)\, XY$.
But the result of these rotations is to map XY onto YX having rotated through a total angle of π. It follows that $\alpha + \beta + \gamma + \delta = \pi$, and the perimeter $= \pi XY$.

8 V stays put and the cone sweeps out a circle of radius l, and centre V. To return to the same spot after 2 revolutions of the cone.
$$\Rightarrow 2 \times 2\pi r = 2\pi\, l$$
$$\Rightarrow \qquad l = 2r$$
Hence α, the semi vertical angle of the cone, is 30°.

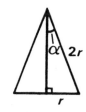

9 As the small diameter is half the large diameter, the cone has been cut halfway between its vertex V and its base.
The cone sweeps out an annulus as it rolls with centre at V and radii 6 cm and 12 cm. The circumference of the cone's base is 8π. The circumference of the outer circle of the annulus is 24π. Hence the frustum will rotate 3 times about its axis to return to its starting point.

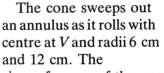

10 Circumference of a roller is 10π cm.

$$100 \text{ km per hr} = 100 \times 1000 \times 100 \div 60 \text{ cm per min.}$$

Angular velocity of roller $= \dfrac{10\,000\,000}{60 \times 10\pi}$
$$\simeq 5300 \text{ rpm clockwise.}$$

11 A moves at 2 m/s upwards
B moves at $2\sqrt{2}$ m/s at right angles to DB.
M moves at 5 m/s at right angles to DM.

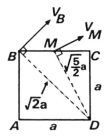

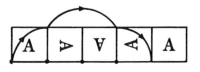

189

13 (a) *C* is the instantaneous centre of rotation.
    (b) *A* moves at 400 km/h to the right
         B moves at 440 km/h to the right
         D moves at 40 km/h to the left.
    (c) All points of the wheel at the same height as *C* are
         moving vertically: to the left, down; to the right, up.
    (d) All points on the wheel which lie on the circle centre
         C, radius 40 cm will have a speed of 200 km/h and
         be moving tangentially to this circle.

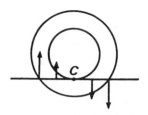

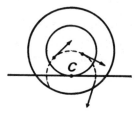

14 The transmission factor ranges from $\frac{1}{10}$, when *W* is
    driving the outside of the disc *D*, to theoretically as large
    as you please when *W* approaches the middle of *D*.
    However there is a limit to the frictional forces available,
    so *W* will slip on *D* as it gets near to the centre of the disc.

15 The transmission factor
    must vary from $\frac{1}{2}$ to 3.
    This can be achieved by
    having the cone *A* with
    diameters from 10 cm to
    24 cm say, and roller *B*
    with diameters from
    20 cm to 8 cm. By making
    the cross-section of roller
    B arcs of circles with
    centres at *P* and *Q* (see
    figure) it is possible to
    design a mechanism to
    move roller *A* so that its surface rolls over the curved
    surface of roller *B* to change the transmission factor.

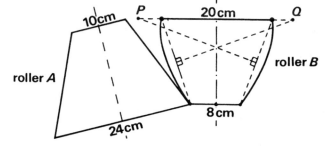

16 Three examples are shown here. One interesting case
    is when a circle rolls inside a circle of twice its diameter.
    Then *P* traces out a straight line, and mechanisms have
    been based on this to generate straight line motion.
    Don't forget to consider what happens when the
    diameter of the rolling circle is larger than that of the
    fixed circle, as in the third example shown.

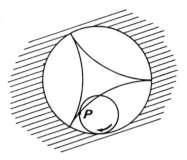

3 - cusped hypocycloid
circles in ratio 3:1

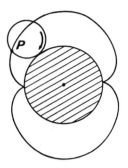

2 - cusped epicycloid
circles in ratio 2:1

epicycloid where the
rolling circle has twice
the diameter of the
fixed circle

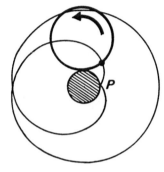

17 $\tan \alpha < \dfrac{d}{2h} \sin \dfrac{\beta}{2}.$

See also *Mathematical Activities*, Activity 66.

Exercise 9

3 Transmission factor $= \dfrac{0.4}{24\pi} \simeq \dfrac{1}{188}.$

The transmission factor can be made smaller by (i) increasing the length of the handle (ii) reducing the pitch.

4 Transmission factor $= \dfrac{3.6}{20 \times 14\pi} \simeq \dfrac{1}{244}.$
Force $\simeq 1220$ kg wt.

5 Transmission factor $= \dfrac{3.4}{6 \times 1.5\pi} \simeq \dfrac{1}{8}.$

6 For each turn of the handle A, D only makes $\frac{1}{4}$ turn, and thus E advances only 0.6 cm.

Transmission factor $= \dfrac{0.6}{32\pi} \simeq \dfrac{1}{168}.$
Force required to lift 500 kg wt $\simeq 6$ kg wt.

7 Transmission factor $= \dfrac{0.2 \times 8}{36\pi} \simeq \dfrac{1}{71}$.

Force at drill tip $\simeq 248$ kg wt.

10 If x is the displacement of
the bolt from the position
where the pin is at the top
of the wheel, then the
motion of the bolt is given
by the graph. The throw
of the bolt will be

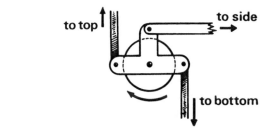

2 × (distance of pin from centre of disc).

11

Exercise 10

1

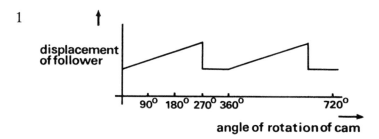

2 Cams (a) and (c) could be rotated in either direction,
but not (b).

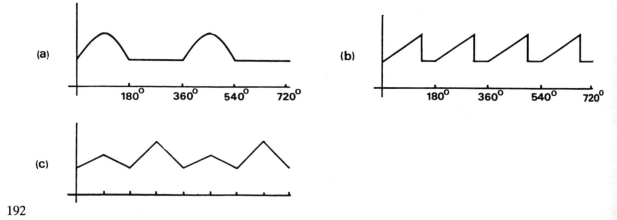

3 The yoke measures $p + q$ by $2q$.
  The follower is displaced a distance $q-p$.

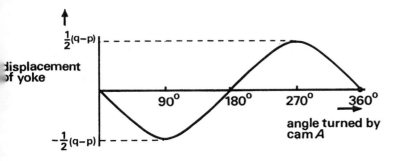

4 Take a circular cam of radius 2 cm and pivot it 1 cm
  from its centre so that $q = 3$ cm and $p = 1$ cm. Then
  the yoke will be 4 cm by 6 cm.

suitable gear train

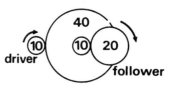

5

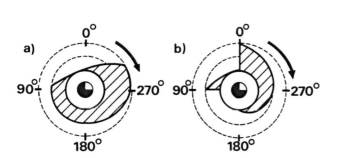

6 A cam as shown in the
  figure, which has
  projections for 120° and
  60°, with 120° and 60°
  gaps, arranged to rotate
  once every minute, could
  be used to operate the
  switch.

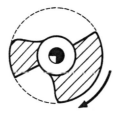

11 (a) 120
   (b) 3 teeth midway between each of the existing teeth.
   (c) by adding a second pawl at 60° to the given one the
       ratchet wheel would never be able to rotate more
       than 60° clockwise.

13 (a) The belt can travel freely to the right but is jammed
       by the roller wedging between the sides of the casing
       as it moves to the left.
   (b) The belt can travel freely to the left but drags the
       roller along the slot and is jammed between it and
       the casing if moved to the right.

Exercise 11

1 (a) 5 times. $Q = 5P$. (b) 6 times. $Q = 6P$.
(c) $\frac{1}{2}$ as far. $P = 2Q$. (d) $\frac{1}{16}$ as far. $P = 16Q$.

5 The daughter would sit twice as far away from the pivot as the mother.

6 Approximately $\frac{1}{2}T$.

8 A moves 504 times as far as b.

If no friction then, theoretically, a force of about 10 000 kg wt is available at B, but a considerable movement from A would be required to produce a very small movement in B.

10 (a) Ratio of areas of pistons $= 64:1$, so B will only rise $\frac{1}{4}$ cm when A is pushed down 16 cm.
(b) 384 kg wt.
(c) $20 \times 64\pi \simeq 4020$ kg wt.

11 (a) (i) $\frac{1}{2}$ as far. (ii) $\frac{1}{6}$ as far.
(b) $Q = 6P$.

12 (a) $\frac{1}{3}$ cm.
(b) 1440 kg wt.
(i) pressure in A and B is 2 kg wt cm^{-2}.
(ii) pressure in C and D is 30 kg wt cm^{-2}.

13 (i) 900 kg wt. (ii) 3 cm s^{-1}.

15 (a) Volume swept out will be $\dfrac{\theta}{360}$ of the volume of a cylinder of radius 6 cm and height 4 cm, that is

$$36\pi \times 4 \times \frac{\theta}{360} = \frac{2\pi\theta}{5} \text{ cm}^3$$

(b) An increase in angle of 5° requires 2π cm^3 hydraulic fluid, so the pump will require a capacity of 2π cm^3/s.
(c) 6 times as far. $Q = 6P$.

Exercise 12

1 (a) (i) 20 s. (ii) 6.
(b) 12 s. (See figure.)
(c) Shortest route along the straight line AB achieved if X, Y and Z components of the velocity are in the ratio 5 : 12 : 3.

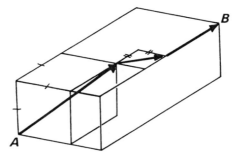

If it is programmed with speeds of 0.25, 0.6 and 0.15 m/s along its axes it will take 2 seconds.

2 (i) $0.02\sqrt{2} \simeq 0.028$ mm.

(ii) $(0.02^2 + 0.02^2 + 0.01^2)^{\frac{1}{2}} = 0.03$ mm

3 Cross-section of envelope is $\frac{5}{6}$ of an annulus with radii 0.5 m and 1.0 m so its area is

$5\pi (1^2 - 0.5^2) \div 6$ m²

and the volume of the envelope will be the product of this area and the vertical travel of 0.4 m giving $\frac{\pi}{4}$ m³.

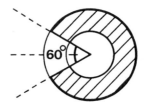

4 (a) To go from A to B, r must increase by 0.4 m, θ increase by 90° and Z increase by 0.3 m. The first diagram shows the relative positions of A and B in space and the sketches give the 6 alternative routes the end of the arm can take from A to B.

(i) Time from A to B is 11 s.

(ii) See diagram.

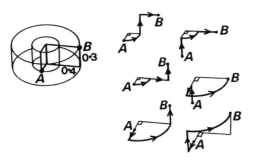

(b) (i) There are 3 stages in the route. The first, when all three joints are active, lasts for 2 s and ends at $P(0.9, 64, 1.0)$.

The second, when only θ and Z are increasing, lasts for 1 s and ends at $Q(0.9, 79, 1.1)$.

The third and final stage, when only θ is increasing, lasts for 3 s and ends up at $B(0.9, 124, 1.1)$.

(ii) Total time 6 s.

(c) A and B are at the opposite vertices of a cuboid with dimensions 0.9 m, 0.5 m and 0.3 m as the change in θ is 90°, hence

$$AB = (0.9^2 + 0.5^2 + 0.3^2)^{\frac{1}{2}} \simeq 1.07 \text{ m}$$

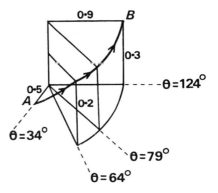

To move the arm along this path would require that the relative speeds of the 3 joints would have to be continuously changed and require a very sophisticated computer.

5 (a) (i) When its arm is only 0.5 m.
  (ii) When its arm is only 1.3 m.

(b) Most of the inaccuracy will be due to a change of
0.1° at a distance of 1.3 m from the vertical axis.
This gives a possible error of

$$\frac{0.1}{360} \times 2\pi \times 1.3 \times 1000 \text{ mm} \simeq 2.27 \text{ mm.}$$

Together with errors of 0.5 mm in the length of the
arm, and 0.3 mm in the vertical travel, this gives a
maximum possible error of approximately 2.34 mm.
This clearly demonstrates the need for a high degree
of accuracy in a revolute joint.

6 (a)

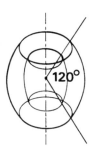

(b) Maximum changes in the joints required are
$\theta \leqslant 180°$ $\phi \leqslant 120°$ $r \leqslant 0.4$ m
requiring 9 s, 6 s, and 4 s respectively, so (i) 19 s,
(ii) 9 s.

7 Start by drawing the
robot's arm in its extreme
position such as AB_1C_1
and AB_2C_2 (see figure).
Then consider where C
can move when B is at B_1,
next consider where C
can move when B is at B_2.
  All the envelope's
boundary will consist of
arcs of circles.

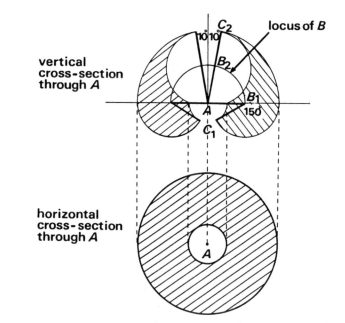

8 As in the previous question, start by drawing the robot's arm in its extreme positions. When B is at B_1 it is important to consider both limiting positions of C relative to B_1, namely C_1 and C_1'. Because BC can only turn 45° clockwise from b_1, the boundary of the envelope at this extremity is rather surprising, but again consists of arcs of circles.

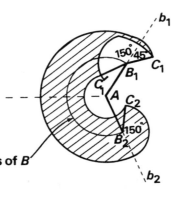

locus of B

1 $y = 2x \tan 10°$. But the effect of the levers means that the jaws move through a distance $\frac{1}{2}y$. So the ratio is $1 : \tan 10° \fallingdotseq 6 : 1$.

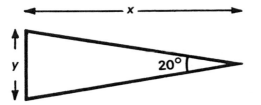

Book references

C. van Amerongen, *How Things Work*, The Universal Encyclopedia of Machines, 2 volumes (Paladin)

I. I. Artobolevsky, *Mechanism in Modern Engineering Design*, 5 vols (MIR Publishers Moscow)

C. V. Durell and A. Robson, *Advanced Trigonometry* (G. Bell and Sons, Ltd)

M. Hiner, *Paper Engineering for pop-up books and cards* (Tarquin Publications)

E.W. Hobson *et al.*, *Squaring the Circle and other Monographs* (Chelsea Publishing Co.)

A. Jarvis, *Hydraulic Machines* (Shire Publications Ltd)

A. B. Kempe, *How to draw a straight line; a lecture on linkages* (Macmillan)

B. Leatham-Jones, *Elements of Industrial Robotics* (Pitman)

D. Lent, *Analysis and Design of Mechanisms* (Prentice Hall)

Life Science Library, *Machines*
Wheels
Time

R. Marshall and J. Bradley, *Watch it work! The train* (Viking Kestrel)

L. Maunder, *Machines in Motion* (Cambridge University Press)

S. Molian, *Mechanism Design, an Introduction Text* (Cambridge University Press)

R. Pawson, *The Robot Book* (Windward)

Schools Council: Mathematics for the Majority, *Machines, Mechanisms and Mathematics* (Chatto and Windus) Modular Courses in Technology, *Mechanisms* (Oliver and Boyd)

M. Sendak, *The Genius of Lothar Meggendorfer. A movable toy book* (Random House)

K. Shooter and J. Saxton, *Making things work* (Cambridge University Press)

S. Strandh, *Machines, an Illustrated History* (Nordbok)

J. Vince, *Power Before Steam* (John Murray)

L. de Vries, *Victorian Inventions* (John Murray)

C. Zammattio, A. Marinoni and A. M. Brizio, *Leonardo the Scientist* (Hutchinson)

Appendix

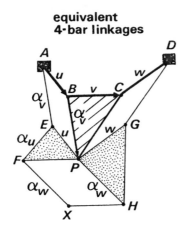

equivalent 4-bar linkages

$ABCD$ is a 4-bar linkage with A and D as fixed points. BPC is a triangle fixed to BC and of interest is the locus of P as the linkage is manipulated. The above diagram is completed by constructing parallelograms, and two further triangles EFP and PHG similar to triangle BPC.

If this completed linkage is made up as a model it will be found that the point X stays put as the linkage is manipulated.

It follows that

linkage $AEFX$ with triangle FPE

and

linkage $DGHX$ with triangle GPH

both give the same locus for P as the original linkage $ABCD$ with triangle BPC.

This can be proved neatly using complex numbers as follows:

Let AB, BC, and CD be represented by u, v and w respectively, and let BP be equal to αv (multiplying by a complex number rotates and enlarges).

Then
$AE = \alpha v$	opposite sides of a parallelogram
$EF = \alpha u$	as EFP similar to BPC
$PG = w$	opposite sides of a parallelogram
$PH = \alpha w$	as PHG similar to BPC
$FX = \alpha w$	opposite sides of a parallelogram

Thus
$$AX = AE + EF + FX$$
$$= \alpha v + \alpha u + \alpha w$$
$$= \alpha(u + v + w)$$
$$= \alpha AD$$

Index

Printed in the United Kingdom
by Lightning Source UK Ltd.
130985UK00001BB/225-236/A